ULITHI

A Micronesian Design
for Living

By

WILLIAM A. LESSA

University of California, Los Angeles

Waveland Press, Inc.

Prospect Heights, Illinois

For information about this book, write or call:

Waveland Press, Inc.
P.O. Box 400
Prospect Heights, Illinois 60070
(312) 634-0081

Cover: A chief executes one of the many formal movements used in the dance.

Foreword

About the Author

William A. Lessa is a professor emeritus of anthropology at the University of California, Los Angeles. He received some training in anthropology as an undergraduate at Harvard but obtained his graduate degrees from the University of Chicago. Most of his fieldwork has been done in China and the Pacific. He was associated with the Coordinated Investigation of Micronesian Anthropology (CIMA) which sponsored the research of so many of the anthropologists who have worked in the Micronesian area. His topical interests include religion and mythology.

About the Book

The design for living carried by the people of Ulithi Atoll becomes sharp and clear in this case study. Dr. Lessa writes in succinct and specific language. He makes no attempt to dramatize. The way of life he describes is so esoteric by Western norms that dramatization would be redundant.

The people of Ulithi engage in a form of ancestor worship. Most of the deceased become ordinary ghosts and are quickly forgotten. Others become prominent ghosts who, through possession of a medium, can provide information on the feasibility of an ocean voyage, the safety of relatives, or the cause of illness. Such a ghost may acquire great prestige over a wide area of Micronesia and exercise significant influence on decision making. On Ulithi Atoll magic is also very important. There are typhoon, navigation, community fish, house, and grave magicians, as well as diviners who can reveal information about hidden events of the past, present, and future.

The Ulithian design for license and restriction in sexual behavior is widely divergent from that of the West. Ulithians engage in what, by Western standards, is a free sex life and yet there are many restrictions applied to sexual behavior. But impotency and frigidity are virtually unknown, and deviant sexual behavior (homosexuality, voyeurism, exhibitionism, bestiality, and so on) is infrequent or totally absent. In general the people of Ulithi regard sex with modesty rather than guilt. Dr. Lessa places the sexual behavior of the people in the context of social and legal obligations and family life, so that its functional interdependence with these other areas of life may be understood.

There are many other dimensions to this design for living. Social and political organization, legal and quasi-legal process, and the entire life cycle from "womb to tomb" are described with remarkable clarity in this case study. But we leave the reader to his own discoveries.

George and Louise Spindler

Preface

You must not seek to find the Ulithi described in this book, for it does not exist. To be sure, you can locate the atoll on the map, and if you can procure the permission of the proper authorities to visit the islands, you will find that there is indeed such a place. But the community as here depicted has undergone such a rapid metamorphosis since my first visits in 1947 and 1948–1949, as well as the later ones of 1960 and 1961, that once I was asked by a young native to clarify a point about the old culture. There might have been some merit in writing a work describing cultural change, but I chose not to do so because I have already written on this subject in connection with a great typhoon I studied in 1961. Instead I have assembled from my field notes, and occasionally from the older literature, a picture of Ulithi (pronounced roughly as if it were YOU-li-thee) as it was when first I went there—projected back, in fact, even a decade or two before that.

Almost all my work was under the generous auspices of the Office of Naval Research and the Pacific Science Board of the National Research Council. If it has been successful, much is due to my great informant and wonderful friend Melchethal, who died only recently. He asked for little (that I order a can of paint for him) and gave much (almost a solid year of time). A man of greater native erudition and integrity I have never known. At least twenty-five or thirty other informants were of considerable help but cannot be listed, except for Iamalamai. He became my assistant at the age of eighteen. Occasionally he writes to me and is my chief link with a little world whose kindly people never questioned my motives or lost patience with my presence. It is my fervent hope that my writings can in some measure repay a gift of human warmth that cannot ever be wholly repaid.

WILLIAM A. LESSA

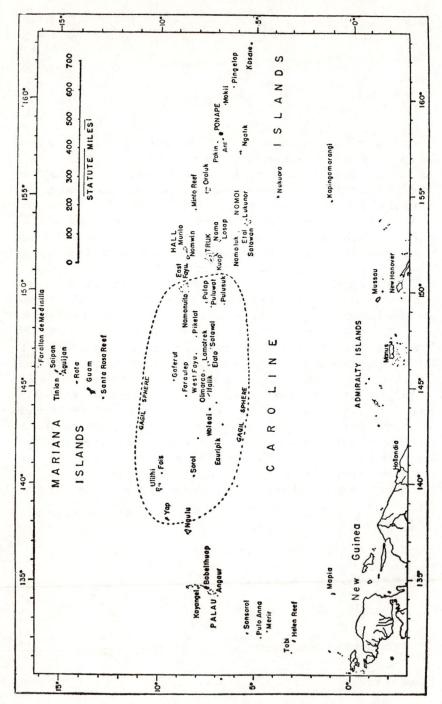

Islands of the Yap empire. Ulithi is in the northwest.

Contents

Above: The men's council on Mogmog, 1948.

Below: A fish magician, on the right, distrains a canoe.

Above: A women's menstrual lodge.

Below: Young adults. They mingle if not within the incest range.

┌─────┐
│ 1 │
└─────┘

Background

ULITHI ATOLL, located at 10°05′N and 139°43′ E (on the island of Mogmog), is a cluster of low islets of carbonate rock near the equator in the western portion of the Pacific. It is the northernmost of all the islands of the Carolinian archipelago, although nearby Yap and Fais are at only slightly lower latitudes. Guam is about 400 statute miles to the northeast, and New Guinea double that distance to the south. If one were to travel due west for almost a thousand miles one would hit the Philippines, an archipelago not unfamiliar to Ulithians who are often stranded there after being lost in the sea.

A Place To Live

Much is revealed about the mode of life of a people to know that they live on an atoll, for such islands are located in tropical or near-tropical latitudes, have little surface area, are composed of calcareous soil, rely heavily on the sea, and support only small populations.

Strictly speaking, atolls are not primarily coral in composition, being built up also from other organisms that similarly leave deposits of calcium carbonate. The corals, however, are a conspicuous feature. They manifest great variety in size and shape, as well as in color; most are gray or white, but many are tinted beautiful shades of blue, green, yellow, orange, pink, and red. It is the skeletons of these fleshy polyps that assist in atoll formation.

Ulithi is made up of over thirty islets, the number being indeterminate for several reasons. Some islets are no more than sandy excrescences out of the sea. Others may disappear temporarily because of the erosive effects of typhoons and tidal waves. Still others, strictly speaking, are not geologically a part of the main atoll. These fine distinctions need not concern us, except that one of the elements usually included as part of the atoll is in fact a submerged atoll in its own right and includes two islets, Gielap and Iar, which have never been inhabited but have some economic and political significance. This element, to the east, will not ordinarily enter into our considerations.

1

It is customary to indulge in poetic imagery when describing the outlines of an island or island group, so one may say that Ulithi looks like a broken mushroom whose stem has been slightly detached from its cap. Although this configuration departs from the ideal circular outline of an atoll, it is by no means aberrant, for fewer atolls conform to the ideal than depart from it. Ulithi's characteristic outline is of course largely a function of the outer contours of the volcanic cone forming the basement foundation of the atoll. More immediately, its shape is closely connected with the reef characteristics of the rim of the island group.

Space resources are tiny, the atoll contrasting sharply with the immensity of the sea surrounding it. The land surface of the main atoll, including the detached island of Falalop, is a mere 1.80 square miles. The largest islet is only a mile long and less than that wide. Yet Ulithi is the biggest of all the atolls in the western region of the Carolines, with a great lagoon or "lake" and extensive zones of living reefs, both of these conditions being conducive to fish production. At the same time its large size is a factor in making transportation and communication time-consuming and sometimes arduous, causing some islets to be relatively isolated from the others. The greatest length of the lagoon is about 24 statute miles and the greatest breadth about 15 statute miles, with a surface area of 183 square miles, a marked contrast to the surface of the land. The maximum depth of the lagoon, 210 feet, places it among the deeper lagoons of the Pacific.

The lagoon plays so vital a part in the native culture that it is well to know that its marine life is greatly influenced by special conditions resulting from its shallow waters and enclosed circulation. The water, which is shallow only by contrast with the surrounding ocean, is circulated mainly by the winds, with additional movements created by waves, tides, and the north equatorial current. The exchange of water between ocean and lagoon is greatest in the winter months when the northeasterly winds, aided by the tides, exert strong action and help effect the exchange of water between ocean and lagoon. One cannot help noticing the stagnant appearance of the water of the lagoon during the summer months, in contrast to the cleaner, crisper appearance of the water in the months of the northeasterlies.

The weather and climate are those characteristic of the Pacific atoll realm, which is to say that there is continuous warmth. Air temperatures, according to a spotty survey, show a yearly average of 83° F, but this may be a degree or two higher than the average over many years. Although a difference of about ten degrees exists between day and night averages, there is little change from one month to another. The mean relative humidity, about 84 percent, is so high that it makes the climate seem very hot in terms of sensible temperature. Clear days are not frequent, a general high degree of cloudiness prevailing most of the time. Fog and haze are virtually unheard of, and visibility is exceptionally good at all times except when it rains. There are occasional thunderstorms, due in large part to the fact that convection attributable to the presence of the atoll is kept down by the smallness and lowness of the land surface. These same factors prevent the production of orographical rainfall.

ULITHI ATOLL

Sorenleng

Lam
Piras
Elemat
Eleute
Ialel Paling
Yareruwachichi

Potangeras
Horaizon
Delesag
Maloiel
Mogmog

Sorlen
Yogoroporapu
Eoet
Asor
Begef
Falalop

Mas

Pogel
Song

Pigelelel
Rorogawappu
Elipig
Songetigech

Mangejang

Lolang

Fassarai

Lossau

Feitabul

Eau
Ealil

Furaza

Pugelug

Pig

0 1 2 3 4 5
STATUTE MILES

While the northeasterly winds and the easterlies are dominant, the winds show a good deal of variability, with the humid southerly and southwesterly winds almost equally as important as these. Ulithi is not in the trade wind realm; rather it is in the typhoon circulatory region bordering the monsoon realm.

Tropical typhoons, which are of course greatly dreaded and have played a large part in shaping the culture of the atoll, may occur during any month of the year, but almost two thirds of them occur in the four months from July to October. However, the two greatest typhoons to strike within living memory came in March (1907) and November (1960). Ulithi is in the incubating area of tropical cyclones, most of which start a few degrees above or below ten degrees latitude.

Ulithians have no strong concepts concerning the length of the solar year but do maintain a system of lunar months. Their primary interest in the seasons is in the changes in the winds, which are so vital for canoe travel.

Topographically, the flatness and lowness of the islets is their most striking feature. Except for the trees, the very highest point in the atoll is on the island of Falalop and is only about 22 feet. Even this is considerably higher than the average for other islands. As is characteristic of atolls, the lagoon shore is lower than the outward shore of each island, and there is often a depression in the middle of an island, which may be converted by the natives into a swamp garden, especially for the cultivation of taro. The shores of the lagoon side of each island are sandy; the opposite sides are rough. Reefs surround individual islands or groups of islands, with channels where the reefs are not continuous. At low tide it is possible to walk from one island to a neighboring island, but the trip is difficult because of the necessity for wading through water about waist high with rough coral under foot. Natives do not often negotiate it.

Water of brackish quality accumulates in the fresh-water lens (Ghyben-Herzberg lens) formed by rain water seeping down through the rock and sand. This water makes contact with marine water that has infiltrated through the porous rock from the sea, and instead of mixing with it will float upon it because of its lighter density. The body of fresh water floating on the body of salt water assumes the form of a lens which is replenished anew by rainfall. On some islands the water is potable, and natives dig wells to reach it. Surface water does not remain standing very long, and that which is held in capillary openings in the soil soon disappears by evaporation and transpiration through shallow rooted plants. Most water for drinking and cooking is collected from roofs and tree trunks when it rains.

The soil, being coralline, does not support much variety of vegetation. While on the atoll I collected a total of sixty-seven useful species of wild flora, this apparently representing the lot, which may seem large but is not. The number of varieties and species of plants that could be successfully cultivated is small.

The wild biota is poorly represented on land. Small lizards are numerous and varied, and there is the very large monitor lizard. Snakes are absent, except for a small, worm-sized burrowing snake that lives in the ground. There are numerous rats, of three kinds. The only other indigenous mammal is the fruit bat, which attains large size. Insects abound. Scorpions, centipedes, and spiders are present but not as common as millipedes.

Permanent birds are few in species; transient birds are much more numerous in numbers and species. The economic value of the avifauna is trivial.

Fish, arthropods, shellfish, and other sea biota constitute the richest group of fauna, numbering in the hundreds, but no effort will be made to name even the more important of them. They have great economic value to the natives.

It would be injudicious to suppose that an ecologic system with the above-mentioned features has shaped the Ulithian design for living into what it is. We must assume that the culture is not a purely indigenous adaptation, and that much of its nature finds sources in antecedent lands. Nevertheless, the environment has offered certain kinds of resources and been devoid of others, and has had at least some say in the way the people can live.

Those Who Stopped By

Ulithi was caught up early in the voyages of exploration made by Europeans searching for a water route to the East Indies after the old route to the Spice Islands had come under Turkish control. We cannot be sure of the first contacts between natives and Europeans, but there is some chance that a Portuguese captain, Diogo da Rocha, was the first to come to Ulithi, the time being October 1, 1525. He had arrived in the Indies via Africa and was on an expedition from Ternate to Celebes, to which the commander of the Moluccas had sent him in search of gold. The problem as to the identification of the islands visited by da Rocha is his failure to locate them longitudinally, for longitudes had not yet been adopted in those days. The latitude is about right.

There are some who think that Ulithi was sighted by the Spaniard, Alvaro de Saavedra, in 1528, as he was making the third crossing ever made across the Pacific by Europeans. The truth is that the islands he saw are in the Marshalls and that he never got to Ulithi at all.

There is much to support the possibility that Ulithi was sighted in 1543 by Ruy Lopez de Villalobos, a Spaniard. On January 23 of that year he came across a small island that appears to have been Fais, a short distance east of Ulithi. He did not anchor there, but the natives came out in boats, making the sign of the cross and saying in Castilian, "Buenos dias, matalotes!" or "Good day, sailors!" He reports that at the same latitude and 35 leagues to the west he encountered another large island, and there is good reason for us to feel it was Ulithi. But who taught the natives to make the sign of the cross and utter a Spanish greeting is a mystery. There is interest in the Fais episode because it indicates that the natives of this area had met and, possibly, for a while entertained a party of Spaniards.

Interest in the Carolines was whetted by the arrival in the Philippines of many shipwrecked natives, some of them apparently from Ulithi. The Jesuit missionaries were particularly aroused by a group stranded on Samar in 1696, and proceeded to make plans to go to the islands for the purpose of converting the natives to Christianity. A frigate financed by the Jesuits was lost in a typhoon in 1698 as it was preparing to leave. Work had to stop because no help was forthcoming from the government, so one of the Jesuits went to Europe in order to procure funds. He was given moral support by Pope Clement XI and financial support by Philip V, king of Spain. A galiot was accordingly able to set out for the Carolines in 1707 but came back empty handed. Another vessel was similarly unsuccessful in 1709 in locating the islands, although it did come close to Ulithi. In 1710 a patache, the "Santissima Trinidad," succeeded in putting some missionaries ashore at Sonsorol but they were killed by the natives while the vessel was away in the course of discovering the Palaus.

Finally, Don Bernardo de Egui y Zabalaga succeeded in reaching Ulithi on February 6, 1712, on the patache "Santo Domingo." The Spaniards induced some natives to come aboard and tried to make them drunk so that they could detain them as guides. They also gave them presents of food, as well as nails, which they seemed to value most. But all the natives except an old man left the vessel. The next day there was an encounter over an effort at kidnapping some young men, and three of the natives were hit by gunfire. The Spaniards then left. A report on the visit mentions, among other things, that the natives "seem to be a very gay race." Another report states that the reception given the Spaniards on their arrival was "friendly," and that the natives treated the visitors as though they were "old acquaintances."

All these events considerably fired up the enthusiasm of a Jesuit destined to be a major figure in the history of the atoll. Father Juan Antonio Cantova, stationed on Guam, where he had interviewed some natives shipwrecked there in 1721, set out for the Carolines in 1722, but after a futile search for the islands his ship was driven to the Philippines and only he survived. The indomitable priest undertook to learn navigation against the day when he would try again, which he did in 1731, arriving at Ulithi on March 2 with a fellow priest, 12 soldiers, 8 cabin boys, and a Ulithian who had been wrecked on Guam. Soon he had baptized 127 children and was proceeding to teach the gospel to the adults. Cantova has left us a fine set of records concerning Ulithi, preparing them both before he left Guam and after arriving at Ulithi.

In May of the same year Cantova prepared to leave the atoll for Guam in order to procure supplies and additional help for his work. He had planned to leave his fellow missionary, Father Victor Walter, to carry on in his absence, but as the vessel was getting ready to sail, he sensed that something was wrong and sent Walter in his place while he remained behind to handle any possible emergency. His premonition was justified. As revealed later, some Carolinians had arrived in the meantime and related to the Ulithians the mistreatment being administered to the Carolinians marooned on Guam. This, and a smouldering resentment already existing among some of the men against interference with their religion and customs, caused them to turn on the missionary party and kill all of them except a Filipino boy. The murders took place on June 9, 1731, ten days after Father Walter had left for Guam. Walter did not return until after he had drifted to the Philippines, remained there a year, had his vessel founder near the Marianas, and spent nine days on his return voyage to the atoll, all of which took two years.

The fate of the Jesuits not only on Ulithi but on Sonsorol before that caused the Church to call a halt to further efforts to Christianize the western Carolines. These two places, as well as many other islands of the archipelago, had acquired such bad reputations among seafarers that they were subsequently avoided. It is a matter of interest that neither on Sonsorol nor on Ulithi is any memory of the Spanish visits preserved in the historical traditions.

For almost a century Ulithi remained forgotten and unvisited. The atoll was again sighted on June 7, 1823, by a Captain John Mackenzie; the event was treated as a new discovery and the islands were named after him. The British captain, who was on his way to India from Mexico after stopping at Guam, stayed only long enough to exchange some gifts and take some soundings, but he did observe that "the natives were well featured, and seemed particularly inoffensive."

Next came Fedor Petrowitsch Lütke, a distinguished explorer leading a Russian circumnavigation of the world. He was interested in Ulithi because it had been shut off since the Cantova tragedy, but his arrival in 1826 came after Mackenzie had already been there. He praised the kindliness of the atollers and noted that they were very timid, although friendly and "decent."

On December 29, 1838, Ulithi was sighted by two corvettes under the leadership of Dumont d'Urville while exploring the Pacific for the French government, but no landing was made.

The significance of these encounters with Europeans should not be overlooked. The atollers were learning something of a vast unknown world from which strangers came with huge vessels, gunpowder, iron and other wonderful materials, artifacts, and ways that were different. Much of what they found out also came from secondhand sources, from other islanders who had seen Europeans. It must not be supposed that between the time of the Cantova episode and the arrival of the later explorers Ulithi had been living in a world sealed off from European influences. The atoll was kept in continual indirect contact with Spaniards through the lively trade being carried on with the Marianas by natives of other Carolinian islands. These natives would return with iron tools, glass beads, and cloth.

Following these first European visitors came the traders, the most important being the German, Alfred Tetens, and the Irishman, David O'Keefe. An anthropologist, Johann Kubary, of the Museum Godeffroy in Hamburg, was a casual visitor about 1870, making some observations on tattooing. Still another anthropologist, the Russian Nicolas von Miklucho-Maclay, stopped very briefly in 1876.

Behind these seemingly desultory events, a pattern of German interest in the area was emerging, and eventually it ran up against the question of Spanish sovereignty, which was tenuous indeed. After several years of litigation, Pope Leo XIII was asked to adjudicate the dispute, and he ruled in favor of the Spaniards, but Germany eventually acquired the Carolines in 1899 after the

Spaniards had been defeated in war by the United States. Ulithi was visited in 1901, 1904, and 1905 by a district officer by the name of Arno Senfft, who left some good ethnological observations. It was during the German administration that a member of the famous Hamburg Südsee Expedition did research on Ulithi, for a little over two weeks in 1909. He gathered excellent ethnographic notes for so short a stay. It was the policy of the German government to disturb native custom and authority in the area as little as possible, although at the same time expanding the copra trade.

The Japanese took over Ulithi and the rest of the Carolines in 1914 after declaring war against Germany. In 1920 they were given a class C mandate over the islands. Because of Japan's military interest in Micronesia, Ulithi and the other islands were virtually sealed off from the outside world. The principal effects of Japanese control were in travel, trade, and education. The administration tried to observe the conditions and spirit of the mandate. As far as Ulithi is concerned, the greatest single impact was on the economy, for the Japanese set up a local branch office for a while to look after the copra and trading interests of the South Seas Trading Company. During this period, some missionary activity was carried on from Yap by Spanish Jesuits. About 1937, one of these missionaries began to make the first sizable conversions to Catholicism among the Ulithians. However, as the tide of war began to turn against Japan after the events at Pearl Harbor, the Japanese attitude stiffened, the two missionaries on Yap were beheaded, and the natives were treated with greater severity than had been the case before.

The first Americans to arrive on Ulithi during the war were troops of the 81st Army Division, landing on September 20, 1944, in search of nonexistent Japanese. They were greeted in most friendly fashion by the people, even though a useless bombardment had killed five natives. Naval military government soon took over and Ulithi was converted into a huge advance base for the invasion of Okinawa and the Philippines. The natives were confined to the islands of Fassarai and Lossau, and given excellent medical and other attention, free from unwanted intrusions by the military. Naval administration continued after the military had left, and was replaced by civilian control in 1951. From that time on, change has been very swift. Ulithi is now a part of the Trust Territory of the Pacific Islands, under the Department of the Interior.

Those Who Came To Stay

It is usual to attribute an ultimately Asian origin to the Micronesians, and there is no reason to dispute this. Contacts with the mainland were apparently terminated long ago. How many centuries Ulithi has been occupied, and whether it has been a continuous sojourn, cannot be said. Tradition has it that the people of the atoll came "from the east." This does not contradict the idea of a more ancient western provenance for the people of the area as a whole, for it is possible that the low-lying atolls were originally bypassed and then occupied by people who filtered back westward. Certainly the people are closer culturally to the eastward-lying islands extending to the area of Truk than they are to the western islands of Yap and Palau. The languages spoken by these eastern islands are mutually intelligible.

Linguistic studies show that Ulithian is a dialect of Trukese, a subdivision of Micronesian, which in turn forms part of the farflung Austronesian (Malayo-Polynesian) language family. It differs sharply from the language of nearby Yap, which, although Micronesian, is greatly aberrant from the nuclear forms of that subdivision. Ulithian is an agglutinative language using extensive suffixes. The grammar is fairly simple and the word order is similar to that of English. Only two verb tenses exist: past-present and future-imperative. The number of consonants is not large but there are many vowels, not always distinguishable to the outsider. Generally, consonants do not follow one another, and one of the devices to overcome the "taboo" against double consonants is to insert an excrescent vowel, such as Mogemog for Mogmog. Accent is fairly even. The language is spoken rapidly but has a pleasing sound. It is capable of being honeyed or whining and may come close to singing.

As Micronesians, the people manifest physical characteristics that have led many anthropologists to think of them as trihybrids composed of more or less equal ingredients of an ancient white strain mixed with Mongoloid and Negroid elements. This is not the place to speculate on the racial history of these natives, who show much variability among individuals, but it is safe to assume that they are closely allied to the Polynesians, although they are less massive and much shorter. Nor, if the hybrid theory is valid, can we say with any assurance whether the mixing took place before leaving the Asian continent, or en route, or even as the result of successive waves. In the light of this, it would be futile to look at Ulithians as embodiments of human racial adaptations to the island ecosystem. Having raised the question, it is best quickly dropped.

Due to measurements and observations taken by me in 1947 and 1948 on fifty-nine males, it is possible to describe the men, at least, with some degree of objectivity. One of the most noticeable features is their small stature, which approximates no more than 5 ft 4⅓ ins. Old-timers insist that in the past the people were much taller, and statements recorded by early voyagers seem to bear this out. Certainly, in the few years that have elapsed since the measurements were taken, there has been an unmistakable spurt upwards, so there might have been a depressing effect as the result of dietary factors. Body proportions, as determined with instruments, show that the men have long trunks, broad shoulders, and narrow hips. The impression one gains is that the men are well proportioned, as well as heavily musculatured and strong. Relying again on measurements, it is found that the head form is longish, with a dolichocephalic index of 74.6. Head size and head height are above what might be construed as average. Noses are broad, but at the same time long.

The skin as described by use of a color scale is seen to be predominantly light brown on the upper inner arm, with a fair share of individuals showing reddish brown and medium brown coloration. The hair is predominantly black, with a moderate degree of dark brownishness. Only in old age does greyness manifest itself. One cannot help but remark on the frequent presence of blond hair among children, which I am inclined to feel is due not to any connection with the blondism reported for the archaic Caucasoid element constituting the aboriginal population of Australia, but to sporadic admixture over the centuries with Europeans. Hair form is mostly wavy, with occasional frizziness and infrequent straightness. Mostly the hair is coarse. Baldness is seldom seen. Facial and body hair is generally small. The eyes have brown to dark brown irises, and I have the impression that the total size of the eyeball is quite large. Eye folds are infrequent, but when they do occur they are usually slightly epicanthic or moderately lateral. The lips tend towards thickness.

There are individuals who give one the impression that they are merely tanned Caucasoids, while others look like frizzly-haired Melanesians. None look as if they were Mongoloids, but many have individual features suggestive of that stock. It is interesting that 45 percent of the men examined had median and lateral shovel-shaped incisors. Dental caries in the males examined in 1947–1948 was markedly infrequent, with almost one third the subjects having all their teeth.

Ulithians are remarkably free of infectious disease. Based on my own observations and some records made by a visiting hospital ship, the following seems to be a fair report. Either completely absent or virtually nonexistent are dengue, malaria, rickettsioses, typhus, typhoid fever, smallpox, measles, and syphillis. There have been epidemics of poliomyelitis during the period of Japanese administration but apparently none since. Intestinal parasites, particularly trichuria and hookworm, do occur and are not uncommon. Tuberculosis, especially pulmonary, is infrequent, although respiratory diseases that do not involve tuberculosis are very common. Yaws, until the advent of the American military in 1944, used to be prevalent throughout the population; its incidence is now zero. There is some filariasis, and its manifestation as elephantiasis can be seen among older men and women. Gonorrhea was unusually prevalent until treated in the postwar years with the newer drugs; now it seems to have been largely eliminated. Deficiency diseases are lacking. I am unable to comment on the incidence of cardio-vascular, gastro-intestinal, neurological, dermatic, carcinomatous, and other diseases. I knew of only one blind man, but encountered no one who was deaf.

Demographic data, although often neglected in research among the simpler peoples, can be extremely valuable in determining not only population size and structure, but other facts vital to interpreting social structure, marital patterns, extent of migration, fertility, and the like. I took complete censuses of the atoll in 1949 and again in 1960 and am able to make detailed reports for those years. However, neither of these times was "typical," for the first census represents a people still in the throes of decline, possibly due to culture contact, and the second shows it in the beginning of a great upward spurt, probably the result of Western medicine. Nevertheless, the figures are not without value in trying to describe what the atoll was approximately like before the disruptions of foreign administrations; therefore, they are offered as crude indicators.

The first thing one wants to know is how many Ulithians there are, and the answer is, not many. In 1949 there were 421 residents, of whom 200 were males and 221 females, but we know that, as with other island populations, there can be and has been a wide fluctuation. Over two centuries ago an estimate by a missionary placed the count at almost 600, and another one made in the opening years of the present century placed it at almost 800. Immigrants have come to the atoll to stay, and about 20 percent of the parents of Ulithians have been counted from other islands of Micronesia. Marriage with persons outside the atoll is stimulated by the strict and wide rules of incest, which often make it necessary for a Ulithian to fetch a wife from elsewhere. Movement into, as well as away from the atoll, has also been dictated by the consequences of typhoons.

At the time of the 1949 census, only five islands were inhabited: Mogmog, 142; Falalop, 126; Fassarai, 69; Asor, 53; and Lossau, 31. In the past, several other islands have had settlements. Ordinarily, the greatest population is on Falalop, the largest of all the islets, but typhoons and disruptions resulting from the war between Japan and the United States have caused it to decline.

Distribution of the population by age cannot be given with the assurance that it is representative, so the figures for 1949 and 1960 will be omitted. It should be said, however, that the earlier sex ratio of 90.5 males for every 100 females was aberrant and suggested the possibility of male infanticide, which in point of fact does not exist. Eleven years later the masculinity ratio had assumed more typicality; indeed, it showed a disproportionately high number of males.

Statistics relative to the marital state of the inhabitants shows that virtually everyone marries, unless he is a psychotic or has some other gravely detrimental handicap. In 1949 there were only seven bachelors and spinsters, all of them with mental or physical defects, except one, who later married. Even after becoming widowed or divorced, there is little disposition to remain unmarried. Age at marriage could not be determined but is only moderately early.

Divorce is common, so that of all persons who had ever married, each had been divorced on an average of 2.05, the figure running to 2.46 for all those who had married and reached the age of fifty or more. The rate of divorce was probably higher in the past.

An inordinate high rate of adoption was revealed by the census, these adoptions all having occurred, as is customary, before the actual birth of the child. The percentage was 45.0, showing only a slight drop by the time of the next census.

Having been told all this, the question still remains: What are Ulithians like? That is, what traits of personality do they have? Fortunately, to the impressions gained from living with them I am able to add the results of Thematic Apperception Tests, or TATs, administered by me to ninety-nine persons of both sexes and almost all ages, and interpreted "blind" by a psychologist. Observations and tests showed much agreement.

These are a mild people who feel and move emotionally in a low key. They experience the gamut of human emotions, including anger, sadness, and pain, and, to a lesser extent, loneliness, guilt, and excitement. Yet they do not give strong expression to their inner feelings. In their thinking they veer away from fantasy and abstraction, and towards the concrete and literal. It can be said that they are not escapists but maintain an essentially ougtoing, optimistic view of life. There is no tendency towards introversion and introspection, brooding and morbidness. There is no sense of vindictiveness. The people do not show a preoccupation with death, nor with suicide, which is something known to have occurred only by hearsay. According to test results, all of which were interpreted in terms of manifest content alone, Ulithians have, as their main goal, food and oral gratification. One might view this as associated with childhood frustrations, but a more likely explanation is that at the near-subsistence level at which the people live they have to exercise a good deal of attention and effort in procuring enough to eat. The tests show less concern with libidinal interests than one might expect. Perhaps one reason for this is that the separate category of amusement really includes the predominant Ulithian notion of "play" in the sense of dating and petting. Certainly, prudery does not conceal concern with sex. As for means to goals, these are dominated by work, group activity, and cooperation. In an atoll ecology, enlightened self-interest demands communality and sharing of work and responsibility. Individuality and personal striving are greatly deprecated, and so are its concomitants—bragging, strutting, and any ostentatious display. This may account for the weak expression of artistic endeavor, but so may the generally concrete attitude towards the environment.

What Is There To Eat

The adaptation made by the people to their environment is limited by pervasive ecological factors that prevent the economy from rising very far above a subsistence level. The small size of the population, the paucity of raw materials, and the simple state of technological competence have worked against the development of a prestige economy. Yet subsistence activities proceed at a sustained and adequate level.

With the raw materials for artifacts limited to little else than wood, shell, carapaces, coconut shell, sennit, and hibiscus bast, it is surprising that so many specialized tools and other objects can be made. Using adzes, drills, and files, the natives make, for example, a large number of kitchen artifacts: scrapers, graters, grinders, knives, spoons, ladles, taro crushers, boxes, beakers, dishes, bowls, baskets, and hanging hooks. Without the help of flint or steel tools, which came in only with the Europeans, native carpenters have been able to fashion good looms, fine houses, and superb canoes.

Subsistence activities are confined mostly to gardening and fishing, with less attention given to the raising of domesticated animals. There is a small amount of gathering, confined for the most part to reef fauna and the products of wild plants and trees. Fowling is inconsequential.

Before devoting our attention to food procurement, some brief words are needed to explain the system of landownership. The system is unusually complicated. This results from the clash of two opposing principles. Matrilineality is seen in the ownership of land plots, whereas a sort of patrilineality exists in the actual tenure of the land. That is, matrilineages have the right to dispose of land and exchange it as they see fit; but they allocate it to individuals who pass it on to their descendants in accordance with a patrilineal emphasis having bilateral overtones. The land plots are of two kinds: those in the swamp gardens and those outside, the latter being much the larger. Boundaries defining the plots are poorly marked, usually by trees, and disputes arise from the consequent ambiguity. Even more serious are the endless disagreements as to rights of inheritance. It is said by Ulithians, with some justice, that land causes more conflict than any other thing in their lives. It is valuable not only for horticulture but, of course, for dwellings, cook houses, work space, and pigpens as well. Certain fishing grounds are owned by districts and there seems to be no problem of trespass from people of other districts.

The staple foodstuffs are certain plant crops. These are simply cultivated.

As in many tropical islands, we must begin with the coconut, which is probably the most valuable tree in the world. Certainly, it is the principal source of food not only for its nut, which is eaten plain or cooked in all stages of maturity, but also for the water in its nut and the toddy yielded by its sap. The planting and servicing of the coconut trees are the responsibility of men, especially since the climbing of these trees is considered inconsistent with canons of feminine modesty. Those trees set aside for toddy do not bear fruit and have to be climbed three times a day to keep the tree bleeding and to collect the sap. The toddy is made into a drink for adults and children, and is nowadays left sometimes to ferment into a wine. Aside from their value in supplying leaves for thatching, baskets, mats, hats, and skirts for prepubescent girls, their trunks are used to make beams for houses, and their roots and other parts to concoct medicine. The flesh of the nut furnishes an oil useful cosmetically and important as a religious and political offering.

Three aroids are next in importance as a source of food. True taro, *Colocasia esculenta,* is grown in swampy pits on those few islands geologically suited for digging down to the Ghyben-Herzberg lens. The cuttings are planted in plots by women early in the morning, and the taro can be harvested in eight months. A long flat digging stick is used to dig up the tubers, which are eaten boiled, as are the leaves. Care must be taken to cook both leaves and tubers sufficiently to dissolve the harsh, glasslike crystals contained in them; if this is not done, the throat can be severely irritated. Magico-religious taboos surround the cultivation of taro, as we shall see in our discussion of things supernatural. The natives have a passion for another aroid, *Cyrtosperma chamissonis,* sometimes known as "elephant's ear." There are four varieties. This, too, is grown in the swamp garden. Less prized but used extensively because it grows so easily is the aroid *Alocasia macrorhiza,* sometimes known to us by its Hawaiian name "ape." It seems to be grown anywhere in the coralline soil and attains great height. Because it is so bitter, it is marinated in palm toddy before being cooked and eaten.

The sweet potato, with nine varieties, has long had great importance in the diet and is highly prized, not only because of its palatability but because it can be planted at any time of the year and harvested within about three months. It is planted from cuttings and dug up with a wooden spade. Cooking is by boiling in a pot, after which the potatoes are mashed into a pulp and covered with grated coconut. Most of the varieties are not sweet to the taste. The leaves of the tuber may be eaten by cooking with an herb and then blending with palm toddy or grated coconut.

Valuable and held in great esteem is breadfruit, which is to be found in twelve seeded and seedless varieties. It does not grow as readily as the natives would like. It is planted without seeming pattern and bears fruit seasonally. The first fruits are the object of ritual attention. Of all foods it is the only one whose preservation is important.

Bananas and sugar cane are eaten raw, but are not important sources of food. They must be cultivated.

Several kinds of wild plants are also sources of food. It is perhaps of interest to know that although pandanus grows fairly well in the atoll its fruit is not eaten.

Some foods of obviously recent vintage are squash, papayas, watermelons, and lemons. There was at one time a tremendous use of squash, which grows well and to great size, but its production has declined in recent years.

All this may give the impression that there is much variety in the Ulithian cuisine, but in point of fact the lament of the natives that their food has a certain monotony is justified. If it were not for food from the sea, things would be far worse.

The utilization of the resources of the sea is easily the most complex of the exploitative activities of the islanders. It demands much time, a variety of techniques and equipment, and great familiarity with the habits and location of the fauna. The proliferation of fishing techniques is necessary for supplementing land-oriented subsistence activities, not only to provide variety and supplementation to the diet but a certain degree of insurance when there is a food shortage, such as follows in the wake of a typhoon.

Spectacular catches come seasonally, when certain kinds of fish come in huge schools to the outer reef and are caught by large numbers of men, working communally, who use long nets to herd the fish together as they wade through the shallow water with the slowly shrinking net. Lagoon fishing is by far the most common of all and has many methods. The most successful involves the cooperation of a large number of men in canoes who assemble in traditional fishing grounds to catch fish with seines. This is the most reliably consistent kind of fishing. Some individuals go out into the lagoon alone or in small groups, using hooks, usually made of tortoise shell or coconut shell, or nowadays steel. Dip nets are often employed in fishing. Some angling is done with gorges made of mussel shell. Composite trolling hooks are used for pelagic fishing, especially to catch bonito, but Ulithians are not fond of leaving the safety of the lagoon, which in any event is the more convenient place to fish. Fishlines are made of sennit or coconut string. Basketry traps and stone weirs are occasionally employed in the lagoon. The traps are usually tied to a drifting log. As much for a sport as anything else, men and boys occasionally indulge in torchlight fishing from the outer reef at low tide, walking along with huge torches whose flames attract the fish, which are then gathered with small nets or clubbed into insensibility. A small amount of fishing is done with metal spears by men swimming under the surface of the sea. Some men fish with throw nets weighted with lead. In further exploiting the maritime aspect of their environment, the women of the atoll engage in littoral shellfish gathering. They also pick up such reef and lagoon fauna as crabs and any fish left stranded in pools by the ebbing tide.

The importance of fishing is attested to by the number of taboos surrounding the fisherman and his techniques, as well as the folklore accounting for the origin of fishing itself. Many of the songs and dances of the people center around fishing, especially of the exciting or hazardous kinds.

Cooking is done in various ways. Thanks to the earthen pots brought in from Yap, boiling and stewing are possible. Roasting and broiling are done on a grid placed over live coals. The earth oven, so characteristic of Oceania, has a prominent place and requires some attention. First, a shallow trench is dug and filled with firewood, which is then burned and superimposed with coral rubble. On top of that are placed coconut leaves, and on these are put the raw food, wrapped in leaves. Additional leaves and mats then cover all these underlayers, and the whole complex is allowed to stand for some time until cooking is completed. Food not prepared in the earth oven is usually cooked in sheds and eaten out in the open. Meals are highly irregular, but usually there is an evening meal participated in by a group which I call the "commensal unit." There are no restrictions as to the age and sex of the members.

Food plays an important part in almost all ritualistic events and is often the only occasion for the event. One does not need psychological tests to realize that nothing makes the people happier than to eat or talk about eating. Only three times over the space of twelve months have I ever seen Ulithians as a community in a state of ecstacy, and each had to do with some huge hauls of fish when thousands of the creatures had been caught by net. On one of these occasions, a fat enthusiast gorged himself with 45 six-inch mackerels, eaten raw, before the formal division of the catch had been completed.

2

Basic Social Relations

THE ULITHIAN COMMUNITY comprises all the people of the atoll, with their common territory, common activities, common interests, and interdependent relationships. Its life is structured and organized into readily recognizable groupings of people who maintain intensely personal and intimate relationships, and experience strong social solidarity. For the most part, the community is locally autonomous and self-contained, but by no means entirely so, for it has a certain dependency on social and political arrangements with other islands. For our present purposes, the wider complex can be ignored.

In the social alignment of the community, it is the village, the family, and the corporate kin groups that are the basic units of social interaction. They will be considered first. Later, other organizing principles of social differentiation and behavior will be considered, particularly the political and religious elements of the social structure.

The Village

The Ulithian village is a highly nucleated subunit of the wider community, and within it its members interact especially intensely with one another, for they are few in numbers and live within the confines of a small area. The average size of a village fluctuates over the years, but at the time of maximum population for the atoll the number of inhabitants for a village came to eighty-eight. That was in 1903. Since then the figure has declined and then increased. There is great difference between the size of the smaller villages and the larger ones.

The Ulithian village, always located on the shore of the lagoon, is compact rather than scattered. Its dwellings are close together and people are thrown into close proximity. This is no place for families who like to be by themselves. The patches of ground surrounding each dwelling are planted in flowers and random crops, such as sweet potatoes, coconuts, aroids, bananas, and lemons. Breadfruit trees grow here and there. Women sit outside their houses,

16

usually in groups, and perform most of their household chores there in the shade of a tree. With them they have their small children, the older ones being at play somewhere on the island, usually at the beach or in the water. Adjacent to each house is a cooking shed of small size and unpretentious appearance.

Canoe houses, better referred to as sheds, line the shore and provide not only shelter for their canoes but a clubhouse for the men of the lineages that own them. Friends often visit them and join in the gossiping and lounging. Some men may be found performing a light chore, such as twisting coconut husk into twine or carving out a loom sword. Children like to dart in and out but may sit still long enough to listen to the conversation and yarns of the men. A canoe shed is a cool place to be, as it catches any breeze off the lagoon and is fairly free, therefore, of flies and day mosquitoes. Men often sleep here at night.

Flanking the villages are the burial grounds, identifiable as clusters of above-surface tombs made of slabs of coral broken off the reef. Cemeteries are simple and unadorned.

The remainder of the island is wooded except for small gardens here and there. Chickens wander into these outer places and scratch around for food. People do not have much occasion to go into the woods, unless they want to gather up some firewood, berries, wild fruits, or leaves. The woods are avoided at night because of a fear of evil spirits lurking there, and if it is necessary to pass through them in the dark, a person will take along some friends and a torch. In the center of four of the islands are the swamp gardens necessary for raising taro, and here a few old women can usually be seen puttering about.

The outer reef is a place for women to gather up shellfish, crabs, and trapped fish. Herons and other marine birds make this their hunting ground. Children seldom play here because the slope is steeper than the repose angle of loose sediments and there is no sand; moreover, it is a little lonesome to be that far from the activities of the village. Men do not have much occasion to be here, except when they engage in their hauls of fish coming in from the sea in schools.

Except for the island of Falalop, where there are two villages, no island has more than one village. The Falalop villages are contiguous, however, and for many purposes may be regarded as a single unit with bonds of common interest. Unless otherwise specified, we shall treat them as one.

The nerve center of the village is the *metalefal,* or men's house. It is large and imposing, as well as conspicuous to visitors arriving from the lagoon, for it is located near the shore in the middle of the village. It has a high pitched roof made of thatch, and is raised well above the ground on a platform built up of slabs of coral. Its very appearance tells one that it embodies the authority and pride of the community.

Its visibility from the lagoon helps guide the visitor immediately to it. And it is well for the stranger to recognize it, for certain amenities must be observed by all visitors, especially those hailing from a land beyond the confines of the atoll. Even passengers in a local canoe returning from a voyage to another island must go through the ritual. As soon as a canoe has anchored, at least one of the passengers must proceed immediately to the house and recite certain words expressing the fact of arrival and prefacing the news that is to follow. To violate this necessary gesture is considered to be an outrageous breech of proto-col, punishable in drastic ways. Should the passengers, especialy if they are visitors, find no one present at the house, which would be extremely rare, they must address their brief ritual, without the ensuing accounts, to any child nearby, and should not even a child be in evidence, they would still have to apostrophize the "spirit" of the house. Usually, however, a canoe is spotted long before it arrives and a group of men will await it, especially so if the canoe is recognized as coming from outside the atoll; in this event the whole village may assemble before the house, with the women and children, however, preserving a discrete distance, for this is a solemn occasion. As the representative of the canoe approaches, even though he may be a member of the community itself, he is met with conspicuous silence and a studied air of indifference, for emotions must be controlled and hidden. There is certainly no hilarity, even among close friends.

The effect of all this is to impress on everyone the seriousness of the arrival. When the passengers come from other communities they tacitly acknowledge by their submission to the rites that they are visitors who hope to be offered welcome and hospitality by the residents. The gesture also serves to inform the village, especially if it should be night, that people have arrived. Failure to go through with the ritual is prima facie evidence that hostile intent or concealment is behind it. However, the main practical effect is the transmission of news. This is supported by the fact that even passengers returning to their own village after a voyage will recite the recent events on the island from which they have come. A villager may have great concern, for example, over the health of a relative, or may want to know if a friend has married or a sister given birth. The strange part of this ritual of arrival is that the opening words are always the same, *"Tor kaptal wai,"* or "My canoe has no news." I found no one who could explain this contradiction and I finally stopped asking. Tradition has a mystique of its own.

Some explanation should be given for the presence of more than one men's house on two of the islands. These are the islands with the greatest population.

One of them, Falalop, has two villages, so there are two *metalefal,* each serving as a clubhouse, dormitory, and meeting place for the men of the village where it is located. But over and above these two is a third *metalefal* whose function is primarily political. Here the chiefs and elders of both villages meet when matters concerning them are to be deliberated upon.

The island of Mogmog similarly had three houses until about a century ago. The main one, called the Rolong, served all the island, which is divided into halves, each of which has its own chief and was probably once a recognizably distinct village. The Rolong served also as the atoll-wide meeting place. Its name is still applied to the site where it formerly stood, and although the house is gone, kings are still invested there. The site has a sacred aura, supported by taboos against trespass and disrespect. No houses may be built on it, so it remains unused, except for an important politico-religious ritual wherein turtles are slaughtered and their flesh apportioned according to a highly formal procedure. Nowadays, the only *metalefal* left on Mogmog is one that in former times used to be simply a clubhouse. The other clubhouse has disappeared, having been destroyed in the great typhoon of 1907, so that the present one consolidates all the functions of the three. It serves also as the atoll-wide council house.

The presence on all other islands of only one *metalefal*, and no tradition of any more than that, suggest that they have never had more than a single village. Each of these houses performs all the functions of both kinds of *metalefal*.

As one walks through a Ulithian village, he will notice that all the houses are built at right angles to the shore—that is, all but one. It is located on the beach and is parallel to the shore. This is the menstrual house, where women retire to have their babies or wait out their menses. Whatever the original reason for this orientation, its position certainly serves to warn the male visitor of its nature and to remind him to observe the strict rules against trespass. Women spend a good deal of time here, and the men often suspect that they use this as an opportunity to shirk their domestic responsibilities. I have heard complaints.

Where there are two villages on an island, there is a menstrual house for each. In the days before the apparent merger of its villages, Mogmog used to have a pair.

This counting of houses, those for men and those for women, may seem tedious and unnecessary, but there is a certain diagnostic value in doing so. Such houses are clues to territorial and political divisions. The fact that the island of Fassarai has two menstrual houses and only one village reveals the rise of an important territorial cleavage there. Fassarai already has manifested a tendency toward bifurcation, as seen in the two named divisions that are beginning to emerge. It is my understanding that the chiefs of the atoll have been petitioned to give assent to the political distinctions that may adhere to such bifurcation.

Further symbolic corroboration of the notion of duality on some islands is to be found in the persistence of a certain kind of house known as the chief's house. Where an island is divided in two, there is a house for each division. It belongs to the lineage which heads the division, and is ordinarily named after the lineage itself. The chief in question is the head of that lineage. The houses are used as meeting houses for the lineages to which they belonged. We know that they also served as meeting places for the territorial division, differing from the *metalefal* in that both men and women could assemble. Despite their loss as formal meeting places, they are still used today on more informal occasions.

Where an island is structured into two divisions, a good-natured rivalry exists and finds expression in competitive dances and sports. The individuals belonging to each half feel a sense of solidarity, and a good deal of mutual assistance is given in the performance of work that requires the efforts of many persons. Cooperation within and competition without find especial expression in two semiannual feasts, one given by men for women and the other by women for men. One division tries to outdo the other in accumulating fish and plant foods for the island.

As a consequence of the frequent and repetitive, as well as direct, social interaction within the village, the pattern of social relations is stable and predictable. The great need for economic cooperation helps shape this pattern, and so does the presence of kinsmen with their strongly structured and almost unalterable social relations.

While the village *esprit de corps* is high it is not unduly exaggerated, and there is considerable exchange with other villages of the atoll. According to tradition, in the past sometimes there was conflict to the point that intervillage warfare burst out. Various forces, however, serve to counteract any real antagonisms between villages. What helps to bind them together in a relatively harmonious single community is not only the mitigating need for economic exchange, but also intermarriage, residence rules, sprawling kin groups, and tributary obligations to the island of Yap.

A further word may be useful concerning the wider cohesion promoted by the rules of residence and of descent. Since these are father-oriented and mother-oriented, respectively, lineages cannot have a real territorial base. That is, even if spouses are discounted, the members of a Ulithian village cannot comprise a single kin group, for although women are the perpetuators of the lineages, they have to move to the residences of their husbands, and this often involves a change of village. To be sure, most marriages take place between residents of the same village, but over the years the dispersive effect of the kind of patrilocality that requires the wife to change villages becomes cumulative.

Countering this centrifugal effect, however, is a modification of the residence pattern, whereby wives who move from one community to that of their husbands regularly return for long stretches of time to their natal villages, principally in order that they and their spouses may cultivate lands that have been assigned for her use through the prevailing system of land tenure. Coupled with a pattern in which most marriages are between members of the same village, certain lineages tend to be identified with one village more than another and for this there are historical factors, for a rule of matrilocality probably prevailed in the past. This is suggested not only by the fact that islands closely akin culturally to Ulithi practice matrilocality or some related kind of residence, but by the presence of lineage houses, hearths, parcels of land, and other things on traditional islands. The transition in residence has obviously been only partially consolidated.

A factor almost as pervasive in social behavior as kinship is the territorial propinquity provided by the village. Exploitative activities are often pursued not by kinsmen but by the village subcommunity, for here large numbers of men beyond the capacities of kinsmen are often necessary. This was hinted at in the discussion of fishing techniques. Again, while the distribution of food at festive rituals is often nominally a responsibility of the relatives concerned, in practice the distribution usually becomes village wide. Once again, some hereditary factors notwithstanding, village political organization is based on the territorial principle, for the group that controls the village is the council of elders, and it is drawn from the entire male membership of the village and not according to kin group representation. In social control, the strength of the village is obvious, for while individuals are curbed by their relatives and punished by them when they transgress the moral code, the members of the village play an appreciable part, through criticism, ridicule, and the threat of ostracism, in inducing them to conform or reform. The village also participates in many of the religious phases of social behavior within the village, even though much of the rest of it is private or kin-based. Finally, the village offers social outlets not possible within kin groups. It permits the exercise of friendship relations, clique behavior, sexual exploits, and such recreational activities as dancing, canoe-racing, and games, in a context providing welcome relief from the often austere character of kinship relations.

The Family

The Ulithian family is based on monogamous marriage, more by reason of economic limitations than moral stringency, for the natives maintain that they see nothing wrong in plural marriages but do realize the inability of a man to maintain more than one wife.

The nuclear family is strongly dependent in character, for it must compete with three other kin groups—the extended family, the commensal group, and the lineage. These other groups assume some of the roles of the nuclear family, which may be, and often is, scattered among other units for purposes of eating and sleeping. Adding to these impinging influences are the extremely common practices of adoption and remarriage. These practices cause shifting about of the personnel of the family, with the result that biological members are often replaced by purely sociological ones. The result of all this is that the feeding, sheltering, training, and other services which the family provides the individual are so dissipated that his nuclear family loses much of its importance in his life. However, it would be wrong to think of it as playing an unimportant role, for the sexual, economic, reproductive, and indoctrinational functions of this kind of family, even though rivalled by other kin groups, are never surpassed by them.

The nuclear family does not usually exist in its ideal form. Attached to it for purposes of residence may be any of various kinds of kinsmen. At the other extreme are residential units consisting merely of husband and wife, with no children or other persons. A canvass of households in the village of Mogmog reveals that only one fourth consist of a husband and wife and their offspring. Almost another fourth of the households are made up simply of husband and wife. The remaining consist of either extended families, composite families, or units not involving a marital pair.

Complicating the picture of the nuclear family is the fact that its members do not always eat together even when domiciled under one roof. In Mogmog's village there are twenty-six commensal units; they do not represent simple combinations of residential units, for an individual may eat in a group in which there are no individuals whatsoever with whom he lives. The average number of people in an eating unit is 5.2. Commensal units tend to revolve around nuclear families, but not invariably so. The members of the nuclear family, then, do not always eat together.

Descent is matrilineal; that is, a child is affiliated with his mother's group of relatives. But this by no means implies that the genealogical relationship with the father is overlooked. Indeed, the father is considered to have more rights than the mother with respect to the child, for in the event of divorce it is he who has custody over him. The effect of matrilineal descent, then, is to affiliate the child with his maternal kinsfolk for certain social purposes but not to deny the genealogical tie to his father's kinsfolk. Accordingly, we find that incest taboos are extended bilaterally, marriages to paternal relatives being forbidden to the same extent as marriages to maternal ones.

Marital residence is patrilocal, a statement that must soon be qualified. The postnuptial location of the couple is with the husband's kinsmen, not necessarily in their household but at least in a dwelling nearby. However, as previously noted, a man must periodically perform bride service for his wife's parents, and if his spouse comes from another island, this may require him to establish temporary residence there. Actually, residence is of an alternating character, but nevertheless fundamentally patrilocal; after the wife's parents die and there is no longer any need to support them, the couple usually goes back permanently to the husband's community to live. This alternation of residence is a concession a man may make to his wife's family when he takes her, a productive worker, away from its midst. However, the matter is not entirely this simple, for the wife may have garden plots in her own community and she and her husband may wish to exploit them for their own interests.

Further clarification must be made of the term "patrilocal." As loosely employed here—aside from the matter of alternation—it does not have the strict meaning of residence by a couple with the husband's parents. Rather, it refers to the tendency for the couple to live in the vicinity of the husband's male kinsmen. When the couple come from the same village, the change is not particularly dislocating for the women; but when they come from different villages, located on different islands, the woman makes a big change. Further complicating the picture is the fact that analysis of actual residence histories shows that in addition to patrilocality as here defined, there is some matrilocality, and also some avunculocality, neolocality, and combinations of these forms of residence. For any given point in time, the mode of residence of a couple may not be what it has been in the past or will be in the future.

It is futile, then, to discover rules of residence from a static census of houses alone. The history of residence must be carefully worked out for each actual case. My own use of the term "patrilocality" is based not on an analysis of the forty-two dwellings on Mogmog, but in terms of the ideal depicted by informants and, even more, the fact that when an intervillage marriage takes place, the wife moves to the husband's community. In addition, we know that when a man's parents-in-law have died he is no longer compelled to spend part of his time living in their village with his wife and children.

Speaking of Kinsmen

The terms used to designate social relationships arising from marriage and parenthood constitute a terminological system of great internal consistency whose character is to a large extent shaped by the system of reckoning descent through the female line. These terms are extended to relationships going beyond the nuclear family. They belong to the so-called Crow type of terminology, and involve not only much use of the classificatory principle but the ignoring of generational distinctions for certain relatives.

The basic kin terms are reduced to a mere seven: father, mother, sibling-of-Ego's-sex, sibling-of-opposite-sex-to-Ego, child, spouse, and sibling-in-law-of-Ego's-sex. The classificatory pattern is seen not only in the overriding of generations but in the ignoring of sex in the term for child and its various extensions. Classificatory terms are also produced by applying all the consanguineal terms, except one, to affinal relatives. It should be noted that only two terms are exclusively affinal. A further reduction in terms is accomplished by ignoring collaterality and merging blood relatives of different degrees of biological relationship to Ego. Put another way, a kin term always embraces secondary and tertiary relatives in addition to primary ones.

Not all societies address a relative by the same term he is referred to, but Ulithi does allow one system of nomenclature to serve both purposes. That is, for example, if you talk about a man as "my father," you then address him also as "father," rather than have to employ some special term.

An explanation concerning sibling terms is useful to know. There really are no absolute terms for "brother" and "sister." Instead, one talks about a sibling-of-same-sex, the term for which is *bwisi*. If it is a male who is referring to his *bwisi*, then the relative in question is his brother. If a female is speaking, she is referring to her sister. So there has to be a term for a sibling-of-opposite-sex. There is one, and when a male uses it he is talking about a sister; when a female uses it, she is talking about her brother. In either event, it's the same term, *mwangai*.

One could easily get to thinking that the Ulithian child has to have a prodigious intelligence and memory to know how he must refer to a relative. Nothing could be further from the truth. For one thing, there are lots of relatives and they are near at hand, so the child has constant opportunity for learning. For another, the number of terms are few, and in any event the child has no need to confuse himself by undoing another system, such as our own, in learning his. The Ulithian system has great logicality and consistency. It follows clear-cut principles.

Nowhere is this better illustrated than in the influence of lineal descent in determining how a relative will be addressed. What could be simpler than to have to remember that everyone in your father's lineage is called your father and mother (see Figure 1). That applies to the oldest and most decrepit man or woman and the youngest baby boy or girl. Age has nothing to do with it. As

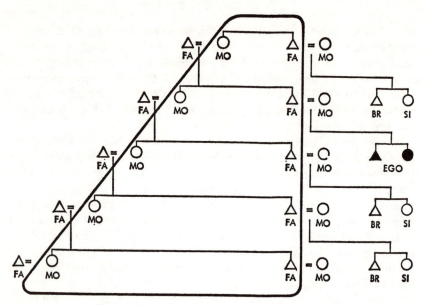

Fig. 1. *Father's lineage (male or female Ego).*

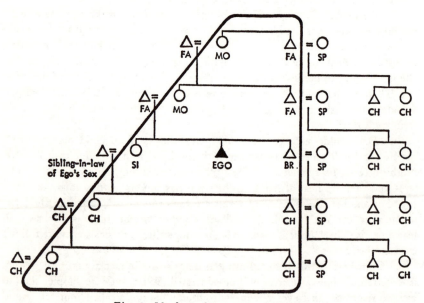

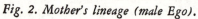

Fig. 2. *Mother's lineage (male Ego).*

indicated in Figure 2, those relatives in your own (your mother's) lineage are known as your father and mother if they belong in any generation above your own, as your sibling if they are in your generation, and your child if in any generation below that. Knowing that, then the people they marry and the children they have are called by terms consistent with the way they are addressed. So if you call a man your brother, it follows logically that you will call his children your children, because brothers are considered to be equivalent to one another. If you call a woman your mother, then unless she is in your paternal lineage you will usually call her children your siblings.

With matrilineal descent the guiding principle in Ulithian terminology, it turns out that certain first cousins on the paternal side are one's parents, and certain first cousins on the maternal side are one's children—at least, terminologically they are.

If the reader has persevered until now and mastered at least the general idea behind the terminology, he may show initial disgust upon being told that in daily life one hardly uses these terms. Instead, one talks about or addresses all his relatives by their personal names, such as "Melchethal," "Sorekh," "Iamalami," "Chuoior," or "Rukhlemar" (which happen to be the names of my chief informants). But all is not lost; the individual has to know the kin terms for each individual relative he deals with. And so, in order to give life and meaning to the system, we may now turn to a consideration of the relationship between kin terms and behavior.

We may preface our remarks by saying that it is axiomatic that behavior between kinsmen can largely be predicted from terminological categories expressive of their genealogical relationship. This is not the place to trace out these patterns in full. They occur in economic activities, the inheritance of property, the relationships within the nuclear family, political status, social control, religious structure, ritualistic obligations, child training, mourning, and many other activities in which kinsmen are expected or required to exercise customary roles. However, at this point we may examine only those kinds of behavior outside the nuclear family that are parallel extensions of sexual behavior within it. These extensions are remarkably consonant with kin terms.

Just as real brothers and sisters practice strict avoidance, so do any other relatives who address one another as "sibling-of-opposite-sex." As long as a man refers to a woman as his sister, he may not be in her company alone, use sexual language in her presence, sleep under the same roof with her, have intercourse with her, or marry her. The number of kinds of sisters falling under these taboos is large: females of the man's lineage and generation, father's brother's daughter, daughter of any man of the father's lineage. But where the biological relationship is actually very distant the rules may be relaxed to some extent.

If a man calls a female his "child," she comes under slightly reduced restrictions. However, as such females are his children, he may not marry or have sexual relations with them, and must avoid coarse language in their presence. Many females come under this category, including, for example, the daughters of his own brothers and sisters, and the daughters of any men in his own lineage. Many affinal relatives too are referred to as "child," but marriage or sexual relations with them is strongly disapproved rather than prohibited. People regard such relationships with ridicule and even some anger. For instance, a man living on Falalop had intercourse with the daughter of his wife's sister, a terminological "child," and his wife became so embarrassed (not over the adultery) that she left him in a rage.

Toward females whom a man calls "mother," the forbidden behavior embraces sexual joking, sexual relations, and marriage but, as with real mothers, does not require the avoidance of classificatory mothers or sleeping in houses other than the ones in which they sleep. This means that there is no mother-in-law avoidance. Relations are thus a notch more permissive than with terminological sisters and terminological daughters. The women who fall within this vast classificatory range, to mention only a few, include parents' sisters and any females of the father's lineage. Affinal relatives classified as "mother" are not as strictly included under the rules, for with such females sexual relations, marriage, and off-color language are considered bad form rather than the violation of a code of prohibitions. An illustration will make this clear.

In an episode related to me by a man, he told of a "son" who was in fact his sister's son. The informant had a young wife and this son had adulterous relations with her, she being his "mother" by virtue of her marriage to his classificatory father. In Ulithi, sons do not make love to mothers, but since the relationship was one through marriage, no incest was involved. But the feelings of my friend were. He was angered not so much by the seduction of his wife—after all, he had dismissed her simulatenous infidelity with a nonrelative as an indiscretion—as by the affrontery of his son, who, incidentally, was older than he. It was a matter of disrespect, and he never forgave him. Umbrage might have lasted indefinitely, except that the offender was later lost in a storm at sea.

It is interesting but logical within the framework of the Ulithian point of view that there is no avoidance by a man towards a female who is his terminological "spouse." Indeed, there is much freedom, as there is with a real wife. He need not sleep under a separate roof from her, although in practice this privilege is not extended except when the husband is away, the idea being that she is better off with him than outsiders. It is all in the family.

Thus, just as kinship terms are mutually correlative or reciprocal in that the use of one term implies the use of another or even the same term, so is the social behavior between the relatives involved similarly correlative and reciprocal.

The Corporate Lineage

Though biological descent is traced bilaterally on Ulithi, an examination of a genealogical chart will usually show a skewing in favor of relatives in the mother's line. This is because there are groups of persons who trace affiliation with one another through females. The most important of these exist in the atoll as corporate groups, which we have already referred to as lineages. There are also a few intrusive, noncorporate groups which we shall refer to as clans. In native terminology, one term encompasses both, but there are important economic and political distinctions between the two, and it is necessary to know when we are dealing with one and when with the other.

The lineage is a group of people with a common name, a common ancestress traced through the maternal line, and an identity beyond that of its constituent members. Its corporate nature is best expressed through the ownership of common property, as well as through its formal organization. The lineage has no totem. It is strictly exogamous.

There are twenty active, landowning lineages in the atoll. There are twenty others that are really defunct but maintained through the custodianship of members of active lineages. In addition, there are some immigrant lineages of recent vintage coming from nearby islands, having no local lands and still maintaining an identity with their homeland. They are represented by a few lone individuals, who sponsor them and look after their interests.

The active lineages are small enough so that the members of each can trace their relationship to one another through actual genealogies, as well as through identification with a traditional ancestress whose name is preserved as founder of the lineage.

Ideally, lineage affiliation can never be changed. Once a Hamathakh, always a Hamathakh. Once a Lipipi, always a Lipipi. But in practice it occasionally happens that a change is made. When a male is adopted he retains the name of his true lineage but interacts mostly within his adoptive parent's lineage. However, when a female is adopted there are complications. She, too, retains her lineage identity, but there is a difference. While the children of the adopted male will belong to his wife's lineage, the children of the adopted female may make a switchover to the adoptive lineage that is complete and permanent.

Most adopted individuals, however, do not change their lineage affiliation. This is understandable when one bears in mind the enormous percentage of newborn infants who are adopted. It would be impossible to maintain any semblance of order if, in reckoning descent, almost half the population were constantly involved in complete absorption into another lineage. An examination of the genealogies of all the people of Mogmog shows that seldom is a changeover made.

Some rank order may be detected in Ulithian lineages, probably having something to do with the sequence followed in the genesis of local lineages through the centuries. The most important unilineal group is the one that furnishes the hereditary chief or king of the atoll, while the next important lineage is that which supplies the headman of the men's council on the island of Mogmog. Their rank is almost coequal. Other lineal groups have varying places of importance, with some so small that they seem really to be sublineages.

The structure and function of these corporate groups are simple and clear. To begin with there is a headman, or leader, known as the *mal,* or male. He is automatically the oldest capable man of the group and derives his prestige mostly from the power he holds in making decisions for the group. His importance also derives from the knowledge of the past that he has accumulated over the years, for such information, especially as it pertains to genealogies and land tenure, is used to back up his decisions. He acts for his lineage when granting or withholding approval for the marriage of younger members. True, considerable personal freedom of choice is permitted in marriage, yet the rules of incest are so pervasive that only a person such as "the man" is in a position to know the sociological eligibility of the prospective spouse. The headman also speaks for the lineage when allocating work and ordering the preparation of food for lineage rituals. He has a strong responsibility, too, in divorcements, especially because of his duty to accumulate the compensatory gift which a divorced lineage mate may be required to give to his or her former spouse upon remarriage. But his main role is in the control and allocation of lineage land and other property.

The female counterpart of the headman is the *fefel,* or female. Her duties and responsibilities do not match his. They include the supervision of gardening, the weaving of fiber garments, and such other tasks as have lineage rather than personal connections. In addition, she has something to say about the marriage of junior members of the lineage. She acquires her position by virtue of seniority, and when she dies or becomes incapacitated, she is replaced by the next oldest woman.

In a society in which there are numerous ascribed statuses, it is not surprising to find that within the lineage there is another kind of position that should not be confused with that of the headman or headwoman. It pertains to generational differences within the lineage. The oldest man or woman in his generation is called by a certain term regardless of sex. Technically, if a lineage had members belonging, let us say, to four generations, there would be eight such persons, a male and a female for each generation. These persons have no duties and obligations beyond a diffuse exercise of authority over the younger persons of their own sex within their generation. Obviously, the very eldest generations have heads who are at the same time the headman and the headwoman of the whole lineage.

Each lineage has its traditional lands. The plots are not always contiguous, for they may have been acquired by exchange with other lineages. But most plots are close together on the particular island where the lineage has its historical seat.

Each lineage also has its traditional house, named after the group, and is the official residence of the headman, as well as the seat of the ancestral shrine. The plot on which the house is built is located within the village proper and is considered to be the most important of all.

Each lineage has its common hearth, where all the members resident in the village eat on various occasions. The lineage hearth does not supplant the family hearth, being activated only when the members of the body eat together on certain ritualistic occasions.

Lineages have their own canoe sheds, the functions of which have already been described. If one were to pick out the place of greatest lineage activity, it would be the shed. This is where things are usually going on.

Tradition has it that in the past, each lineage had its own menstrual house. Such individualism has now given way to communalism.

A very important piece of property, the canoe, always belongs to a lineage, unless it is small and without sails. Some lineages have as many as three canoes, whereas others are so small that they have none of their own. A superficial observer might get the erroneous impression that canoes can be used freely, and that when a man wants to go somewhere he simply puts out to sea. Nothing could be further from the truth. The lineage engages a man, who may not even belong to it, to look after the canoe and grant permission to those who wish to use it. Such borrowers may not even be members of the group, having to make their request because their own lineages have no boat available. The carpenter who constructs the canoes may not be a member of the descent group, either, having merely been commissioned to do the job. The headman is the one who decides when a canoe is to be built and when a new pandanus sail is to be woven by the women of the lineage. He has the curious responsibility of making the sennit rope used on a canoe, but no one knows the origin of this obligation. As a reward for this ritualistic chore he receives two fish from any catch made by the users of the canoe if it has been in private service; otherwise, he receives none.

Finally, each functioning lineage has its pool of ancestral ghosts and a shrine for the sacrifices made to these spirits. The shrine is in the traditional lineage house and is cared for by the headman, who receives the offerings.

The profound importance of lineal descent groups should at once be obvious. A person owes much of what he is and what he can do to his membership in a lineage.

By contrast, the clan in Ulithi is of little consequence. Clans are intrusive and unimportant locally. They are noncorporate and unorganized. They do not have a local clan hearth, house, headman, or shrine, nor do they possess their own canoes or ghosts. The members of each of the six clans represented in the atoll bear a common name with alleged common ancestry from such animals as the porpoise, eel, rat, and a shellfish. That is sufficient to make the clan exogamous. Members of clans fit into the Ulithian scheme of things by becoming absorbed into local lineages, which is done either through marriage or adoption. In time, such people may take over a moribund lineage and completely control it and its lands, at the same time dropping their old identity in favor of the new. The hospitable acceptance of clan members into Ulithian society is further testimony to the tolerant and outgoing nature of the natives.

Relatives Right and Left

Figuratively speaking, and following the structure employed by genealogical charts, people have maternal relatives on the right-hand side and paternal relatives on the left. Can we in any sense think of them as a unity?

Yes, but not in the sense that they are a discrete group. They are a unity only as a category—a category of cognates or persons related to an individual by ties of blood relationship, affinals being excluded. Ulithians call these kinsmen the *ieremat*. In a society in which the principle of descent is unilineal it should not be overlooked that recognition must be given to kinship ties on both sides.

Ulithians do not precisely define the members of one's kindred, who, theoretically, are all the people who are his cognates. In practice, out of this vast pool only the following are usually included: one's parents and their parents, one's parents' siblings and their children, his own siblings and their children, his own children and grandchildren, and the members of both parents' lineages, unless they are distantly related. Cognatic kin of this sort lack a corporate character because of their inherent inability to perpetuate themselves as a formal and autonomous group. Because the *ieremat* shift composition for any individual and his siblings, they have fixity only for Ego.

Since the kindred cannot perpetuate itself as a body, it cannot have a house, headman, headwoman, ancestral shrine, or property.

Yet, for Ego, the kindred is real. He knows that he cannot marry anyone within this category, and that relatives on both sides will assemble and come to his aid when necessary, or participate in some rite on his behalf. At the same time they will criticize his behavior when it merits criticism. Members of the *ieremat* have a hand in raising him and when he visits any of them they make him feel welcome to food, shelter, and any other kinds of hospitality. They will present him with small gifts on such occasions. When the individual needs labor to complete an enterprise they stand ready to assist. Obviously, these cognatic relatives have functions duplicating or overlapping those of the lineage, but they are real roles, performed by a fairly well-defined group.

In conclusion, Ulithian society is not bilateral, but within its unilineality it provides ample room for noncorporate kin groups drawn from all the individual's cognates. It has seemed necessary to point this out lest one gain the impression that no social function adheres to biogenetical consanguinity.

3

Political Organization

CONSIDERING THE SMALL SIZE of the territory and its population, the political system of the atoll presents unexpected complexity. Some of the complications are due to the political overlordship of nearby Yap, for this dominance shapes the local organization in a fashion designed to make it mesh with the caste and landownership system of the Yapese.

There can be little doubt that viewed from the historical perspective the Ulithian system of government grew out of a kinship foundation. This accounts for the mildly gerontocratic tinge to political power, for political officers and representatives are drawn from lineages in accordance with the principle of seniority. At the same time it accounts for the strongly democratic nature of political authority, for all lineages have some voice in government, at least in internal affairs.

The political system is so influenced by kinship principles that at many points it tends to become identified with it. One notes that at the level of local government, quasi-political authority is lodged with the family and the lineage. Each exerts great social control over its members and acts as an informal punitive body. In addition, the lineage regulates marriage, land tenure, and various other matters affecting its members. The *mal,* or lineage headman, is the instrument for the exercise of whatever political power is held at this level. It is he who calls meetings of the lineages and presides over them.

But true political organization is not encountered until one goes beyond the kin groups and examines the way in which villages, districts, and the whole atoll are administered.

The Village Council

The everyday affairs of a village rest in the hands of a council of elders. This body is headed by a chief known as a *metang.* To become a member of the council requires no qualifications of wealth, lineage, heredity, or anything more

31

than middle age and a measure of intelligence and responsibility. Young men are not admitted into the deliberations of the council, unless hereditary factors have already caused them to become district chiefs. There is no objection, however, to any man's sitting to one side as a spectator. No formal action or ritual is involved in becoming a member of the council. It is merely a matter of tacit understanding and assent.

The council meets several times a week, sometimes daily, in order to confer on community affairs and reach decisions. Its deliberations are concerned with economic and political matters, such as catching fish, constructing and repairing council houses and menstrual huts, policing the island, and any other tasks requiring communal effort on behalf of the whole village. The council also acts when it receives orders emanating from higher authority, either inspired locally by the paramount chief or relayed by him from sources outside the atoll, usually Yap. The *metang* presides over meetings, and does so with impartiality, dignity, and decorum. He allows free discussion by members and is guided and corrected by them. But if he has a strong personality, he may greatly influence the decisions ultimately agreed upon by shaping the agenda and the discussion along lines that he knows are compatible with the wishes of the district chiefs and the king; but as a rule these latter are above the relatively routine matters being dealt with, and so remain passive.

The *metang* can be a dynamic and influential leader, but since he attains office by virtue of membership in a traditional lineage he may be weak and ineffectual, so that the people of the village will have to put up with him until he retires of old age or dies. It is unthinkable that an incompetent man should be ousted, especially if he has not yet fallen into the decrepitude of the aged.

The council is a hardworking body, highly sensitive to the common good. Every effort is made at fairness. Thus, the *metang* is always drawn from a different village from the district chief, so that a balance of power can partially be maintained. Individual members are heard with respect, and there is no shouting or excitement. Ulithians are fond of decorum. A person with a desire for fame has no place in the society and would be withered with silence should he disport himself with passioned oratory or anything else that might appear to be ostentatious.

The District

Beyond the village, the next larger political unit is the district, of which there are eight in the atoll. The district is composed of a village and one or more lesser islands, most of them uninhabited but nevertheless economically useful.

Each district, including some that are no longer inhabited, is headed by a chief. His jurisdiction does not extend over any village in his area but rather over the district as a whole. The nature of this jurisdiction is vague but is principally concerned with the interests of the district as a whole in matters involving the entire atoll. A district chief, as such, does not have the right of eminent domain over the land that he controls politically, although he may exercise such control if he is simultaneously a landownership chief.

Succession to chieftainship is matrilineal and occurs through certain hereditary lineages. The oldest male member succeeds any chief who dies or becomes incapacitated, but Yap must give its approval to the succession.

Districts, which bear no names and are identified only by the name of the principal island dominating each, are ranked in a crude fashion that does not seem to follow any consistent principal. Mogmog is at the top, which is understandable, but the districts of Mangejang and Sorlen, which are relatively unimportant, come next, each being co-equal in status with the other. At the third level comes Falalop, with both Fassarai and Lossau occupying a fourth order of rank. Finally, at the bottom are Losiep and Asor. A definite chain of authority exists among these districts and this is tangibly expressed in the way in which orders at the top are transmitted to inferior districts by envoys. These messengers, or envoys, are men of chiefly status and follow a pattern that need not be discussed here. The rank order of the districts has its origin in the past and cannot be explained. Propinquity or considerations of transportation do not enter in, for some of the lower ranked districts are nearer to Mogmog than are some of the higher ranked ones.

No larger units than the political districts exist on the atoll; however, there are two other kinds of districts, one pertaining to landownership and the other to the caste system of Yap. The functions of these are not truly political.

Most likely, district chiefs, like other chiefs, commanded great respect in the past and a certain degree of subjugation. Father Cantova, observing castaways who had reached Guam from the general area, wrote in 1722 before going to Ulithi that their chiefs "govern with authority, speaking little and affecting a grave and serious air." When a chief granted an audience he sat on a raised table, and the people approached him bowed almost to the ground. "His words are as so many oracles that are venerated; a blind obedience is rendered to his orders." When some favor was asked of him the people kissed his hands and feet. Mind you, all this was on Guam where the Carolinians were virtually prisoners of the Spaniards.

It is not likely that chiefs on Ulithi, or nearby islands, have manifested such marks of regality for some time. Foreign domination through aggressive traders, such as O'Keefe, or through government control, as after the Germans came in, probably irrevocably undermined the splendor and power of the chiefs. Unfortunately, when Father Cantova got to Ulithi in 1731 he failed to speak of the chiefs and their lofty status. But when pieces of evidence are carefully assembled, the picture they present is one of a "nobility" approximating that of the Polynesians.

Chief of Them All

Ulithi is under the jurisdiction of a paramount chief, referred to in a loose way by Europeans as a king. He has some judicial authority but exercises it moderately. As executive head of the atoll he exists mostly to coordinate atoll-wide affairs and preserve interdistrict harmony. In most instances, he does not originate many orders, leaving the affairs of the people mostly to their own lineage chiefs and village councils. The outstanding exercise of his office is in external matters, principally involving relations with Yap and other islands of the western Carolines. When grave matters are to be settled he summons a kind of supercouncil made up of chiefs representing each of the villages and districts. The deliberations are conducted in the same democratic and restrained manner as in meetings of the village council, with the paramount chief seeking to gain a consensus of his subordinates. The council house on Mogmog is of course the forum for these discussions.

Succession to the paramount chieftainship is hereditary within the Lamathakh lineage. The man who succeeds to office is ordinarily the oldest son of the oldest daughter of the outgoing head, unless the latter has a younger brother to succeed him. A king cannot, of course, pass on his office to a son since his children never belong to his own lineage.

One would hardly think that so tiny a community as Ulithi would have a "coronation," but it does and it is both solemn and religious. Before the investiture, the consent of Gagil district in Yap must be obtained, consent seldom being denied. After endorsement from Yap, the district chiefs of Sorlen and Mangejang are notified through envoys, and these chiefs in turn notify all other chiefs and lineage heads throughout the atoll that a convocation is to be held. The assembly is not designed to express endorsement of the candidate but only to witness and participate in the investiture.

The ritual involves certain spatial arrangements of the participants, with the chiefs and headmen gathered in a circle in front of the atoll-wide council house on Mogmog known as the Rolong, and the spectators, always males, seated behind them. In the center of the circle sit the two chiefs from Sorlen and Mangejang. On this occasion, only they are allowed to wear the combs that distinguish chiefs from others, fastening the feathers of a black bird to the comb. By prearrangement, one or the other of these chiefs officiates. The incoming king is placed in the center of the circle with these two men. The officiating chief begins the ritual by holding up a special type of loincloth over his head and, addressing the great spirit of the Sky World, Ialulep, and the great spirit of the Earth World, Solal, announces to them that a new king is being installed. He implores these great gods to give long life to the chief should he rule well, but to cause his death should he rule badly, so that he may be replaced by someone more worthy. The ceremony is brief but by this simple gesture and these few words not only is a new king inducted into office but he is at the same time transformed into an individual of sacred character who henceforth must live a life apart. The special loincloth, accepted but never worn by him, is disposed of in any way he sees fit, often being sent to the paramount chief of Gagil district in Yap as a token of good will.

Upon assuming his new status, the paramount chief has to live an ascetic life, being enjoined for five years from sexual relations and from sharing his food with anyone else. Afterwards, he is allowed to share his food only with religious specialists of the highest order—diviners, typhoon magicians, fish magicians, and navigators. At no time may he eat food prepared by women still in the menarche. Many more taboos give testimony to his sacred nature. No one may share his drinking water, coconuts, palm toddy, tobacco, turmeric, and coconut oil. His palm toddy may be collected from his trees only by the major religious personages; all others are forbidden to touch the trees. No one may sleep in the same house with him, except his wife, and then only after the original period of taboo against coition has expired. In fact, no one else may even enter his house except the religious specialists and the woman who cooks his food. During the five-year period of taboo no one may so much as touch his person, and even after that he may not be touched by children, young men, or women who have not reached the menopause. Perhaps the most conspicuous concession to his high status is the requirement that all persons walking past him must crouch or crawl, calling out the words *"Soro! Soro!"* as they go by. To be sure this gesture of respect is required toward all chiefs but they themselves do not perform this gesture to anyone else except the king. The five-year period of taboo obviously imposes considerable inactivity on the paramount, for during that time he may not work, or climb trees, or dance, except solo. However, he may fish. One kind of fish, *hathekh* (unidentified), is reserved exclusively for him at all times. It should be apparent that the investiture and the observance of the taboos endow him with an aura that goes a long way towards maintaining his position of authority and responsibility.

Relations Without

This seemingly tight little world is in reality enmeshed with many other islands of the Carolines. Interaction with some of them is informal, but with the great majority it is structured along hierarchical lines, in which not only political but economic and religious factors play a part. The islands with which these formal relations are maintained lie within the domain of Gagil district on Yap. They constitute a miniature empire.

Does this mean that Ulithi is not a state? This depends on your point of view. The political entity that is called the state has been defined in many ways. Some insist that it be exclusively invested with the final power of coercion. Others stress the delegation of power and control to a few members of the society. In both instances the idea of force is never far away. The approach I favor is one that thinks of the state as a sovereign territorial group. How does Ulithi meet this succinct definition? Certainly, without stopping to argue whether or not the enforcement of rules is a function of a differentiated system or organs within the community, Ulithi is a human group, having a distinct territory, and possessing a government of a sort. The crucial question is whether it has sovereignty. In general, yes. Yap steps in to threaten and demand, but it is significant that Yap does not perform what is the chief function of the state—the maintenance of social order. Yap has almost nothing to do with internal events in Ulithi; it is mostly concerned with relations between the two communities.

In view of this, the dilemma may perhaps be resolved by thinking of the atoll as a satellite state.

From the point of view of Ulithi, as told to me by knowledgeable old men there, the Yapese empire may be seen as constituted of three blocks: Yap (Gagil district), Ulithi, and the Woleai (see Figure 3). The name "Woleai" is the one given by Ulithians to all the islands to the east, except nearby Fais, that form part of the Yapese sphere. These islands are subordinate to Ulithi, and both these units are in turn subordinate to Yap. Ulithi generally acts as an intermediary. How Yap came to control these islands is a mystery lost in the distant past.

To start with Yap, it is necessary to know that there exists internally in those islands a strong caste system in which the upper caste controls the lands used by the lower caste. Marriage between the two groups is forbidden.

What the Yapese have done is extend their caste system to Ulithi, so that Ulithians are serflike inferiors who may not intermarry with the Yapese and must at the same time send them political tribute, as well as payment for use of their own land and as offerings to certain spirit beings. In this system, the Yapese are known as "fathers" and the Ulithians as "children," a fictive kinship terminology also employed between the two Yapese castes. Much of the behavior between the people of Gagil district on Yap and the people of the atoll is epitomized by these terms, for the former are under a certain kind of obligation to look after their so-called children, while the children are obligated to show respect and gratitude towards their parents. The relationship may be described as symbiotic to the extent that it involves reciprocally advantageous relations between dissimilar participants. If anything, the inferior unit has more to gain than to lose through the arrangement.

Yap exercises indubitable political control over Ulithi. It demands and receives tribute in the form of mats, rope, fine textiles, and food. This tribute goes only to the paramount chief of Gagil district, although in accordance with the prevailing system of economic distribution it eventually finds wide distribution throughout Yap as gift exchange. The demands from Yap for tribute, which comes about every two or three years, follows a regular chain of authority, being given first to the paramount chief of Ulithi and then, through him, to the chiefs of the various political districts of the atoll. Protocol must be strictly observed in communicating the demand, with envoys meticulously consulting the proper lineage heads and the districts they represent. Political tribute is not given regularly but may be ordered on any one of the annual visits to Yap required of the paramount chief of Ulithi.

An aspect of dominance that has greater practical significance in the economic sphere is the payment by Ulithians of a kind of rent to certain lineages in Gagil district. Ulithians are considered to be tenants of land owned by absentee landlords in Yap. The Ulithian lineages are locked with those of Yap in what is known as a *sawei* relationship, and although the precise etymology of the word is not known, it refers in effect to not only the system of tenancy but to the kinship units involved, as well as the goods exchanged. The word "exchanged" is used advisedly, for after the tenants have delivered their payments of foodstuffs

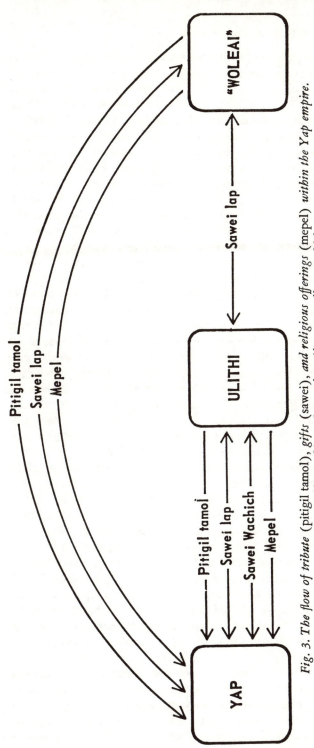

Fig. 3. *The flow of tribute* (pitigil tamol), *gifts* (sawei), *and religious offerings* (mepel) *within the Yap empire. Some gifts are big, or lap; other gifts are small, or wachich.*

and goods, they are given return gifts by their landlords, and these often, if not usually, exceed the payments! Because of this reciprocity it is hard to justify use of the term "rent" but the fact remains that while payments made by tenants are obligatory, the gifts given in return are optional. Ulithians usually find the arrangement so much to their advantage that they do not mind humoring the Yapese by calling them fathers or mothers and being called children in return. Nor do they mind too much the restrictions imposed on them when they visit Yap, for when they go there they are given shelter and food and permitted, if they so desire, to build canoes using the large local mahoganies lacking on the atoll. In return, they must show deference, refrain from making sexual advances towards Yapese women, observe numerous food taboos, and perform a certain amount of work. Some might find this degrading, but people living on impoverished islands do not find the choice difficult to make. Yap is a land of variety and abundance, and going there is a kind of exciting adventure for people who live on tiny, flat islands devoid of many resources.

The subordination of Ulithi is further seen in a final kind of tribute that must be sent to those lineages on Yap with which the atoll lineages are paired in the *sawei* relationship. These are religious offerings made to the lineage ghosts of the Yapese. It is not clear why people with their own ancestral ghosts should have to send coconut oil, pandanus mats, and finely woven loincloths to alien spirits. However, it has been suggested that since Yapese lineage ghosts are beneficent not only towards their own descendants but the wards of their descendants as well, the Ulithians should be acting out of gratitude for the services rendered by such ghosts. Mitigating the necessity for making these religious offerings is the fact that the major one of the ghosts is claimed by Ulithians to be one of their own—at least he was born on Ulithi, of a Yapese mother.

There remains the connection between the second and third units of the Yap-Ulithi-Woleai complex, and here we find some replication of the above scheme. Certain Ulithian lineages are the parents and landlords of the filial islands of Fais, Sorol, Earipik, Woleai (atoll), Ifaluk, Faraulep, Lamotrek, Elato, Satawal, Puluwat, Pulap, Pulusuk, and Namonuito (see Figure 4). These eastern islands must give *sawei* to Ulithi and in turn they receive gifts and hospitality. There is no implication here of caste; indeed, intermarriage between Ulithians and these neighbors is frequent and relations fairly relaxed. All indications are that the replication has its source in Yap's ultimate political control over the islands of Woleai, in which Ulithi acts as intermediary between the first and third units by looking after the interests of the lineages of Gagil district. Ulithi's right to *sawei* from the eastern islands seems to be compensation for its administrative services.

Replication does not extend to political tribute and religious offerings. True, Woleai must send these to Yap but Ulithi's role is simply to pass on orders for them and supervise their transportation. This is done according to a strict chain of authority that is scrupulously observed, so that a small island will not comply with orders from Yap unless they have been sent in accordance with the proper pattern. The importance of Ulithi's position is better understood

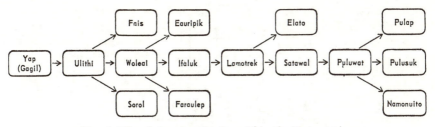

Fig. 4. The chain of authority within the Yap empire.

when it is realized that there is no direct communication between chiefs on Yap and the Woleai.

Turbulence occasionally marks Ulithi's relations with Yap, usually over sexual rivalry and the breaking of taboos, but also over real or imagined insubordination. Since Yap always holds the ultimate upper hand in the form of natural resources not found in the atolls, it prevails. But when the symbiosis is working smoothly, which is to say when the children are showing proper respect and gratitude towards their parents, then the people of the atoll have the advantage. For, to repeat, in this whole relationship the upper caste usually exercises a benevolent paternalism over the lower caste. From the point of view of the Ulithian, where else can he get yams, betel nut, Polynesian chestnuts, big timber, ochre, and other prized goods? Not unless he were to risk distant voyages of hundreds of miles instead of a mere eighty-five, and then he would not be sure of success for his efforts. He would have little more to offer in return except services in transporting goods in their own canoes.

Evidence of the persistence of the Yapese empire over time comes from the pen of Father Cantova, who, writing in 1731 from Ulithi, stated: "These islands [Ulithi] like so many others of this archipelago are subjects of the king of Yap."

Outside this political complex there are other islands, and Ulithi has intercourse with many of them, particularly Ngulu, where many Ulithians settled some time ago. Contacts are maintained, too, with Sonsorol, Pulo Anna, Merir, and Tobi, a group of distant atolls where some Ulithian lineages are represented. Occasional visits are made to Truk and Palau. Ponape and Kusae are known mostly by name. The Marianas have some affinities with the atoll on account of the refugees once located there after a typhoon, but also because of contacts established centuries ago. But political influence is entirely lacking once one leaves the Yapese sphere.

There are traditions of warfare between islands. These apply to a period too remote to speak of authentically. Yet warfare has existed and cannot be discounted as one of the characteristics of this island world.

4

Aspects of Law

I N ADDRESSING OURSELVES to the question of law we are not interested merely in customs or morals but in those social norms whose violation invokes the use of systematic and coercive procedures of formal nature. Ulithian modes of conduct which are legal, or at least incipiently legal, cannot however always be clearly distinguished because they do not conform to law in the sense that it exists in more complex societies.

The Stuff That Makes Law

In a society that values conformity and deprecates controversy, there is little opportunity for law to be formed, for law requires the processes of litigation for its development. The truth is that contentiousness is not favored by the mores of the people.

I am reminded of a comment made by a young Ulithian who, after considerable hesitation, consented to relate to me the details of his recent divorce. On asking him what proof he had had of his wife's infidelities, he replied that after receiving hints from reliable sources he had crept up one night outside the house where he knew that she and a young man were alone. He heard enough to know positively that they were engaged in the most ardent of intimacies. I pressed him to recount what had happened next. "I went home," he said. I protested that in America he would probably have burst through the door and assaulted the lovers. No, he insisted, that would have been bad. "When my wife came home I told her she must stop doing this. I did not speak to the man about it." There is not much chance for law to be formed in an atmosphere of such exquisite restraint.

If litigation is weak, the answer is to be found in the structure of the society and the whole way of life. The relationships that people have to one another have been worked out over many years and are predominantly personal and kinship in character. The thrust for conformity comes mostly from outside the law, for the very nature of legal procedures and sanctions is contrary to the prevailing spirit of so minuscule a society. Pressure to conform of course comes in part from the dread of criticism, public contempt, ridicule, and ostracism.

It comes also from the sheer need for cooperation. In an insular environment where life is not easy to sustain and the catastrophic effects of typhoons are always menacing, one cannot dare risk the loss of the reciprocal aid so needed to carry on. Conformity is vital for economic activity, which has a highly cooperative character in the atoll. But it has other rewards: companionship, affection, and status. The pressure to conform comes mostly from one's kinsmen, for they above all others offer not only these inducements but food, clothing, shelter, and property rights as well.

Finally, pressure to conform comes from the fear of supernatural retribution. It might be insisted that the punishment of delicts by supernatural agencies is actually a part of Ulithian law. While it is true that such punishment serves as an important force of social control, it is by no means to be construed as a kind of law. Even though the sanctions of supernatural agencies are thought to bring about misfortune, illness, or death, they do not involve procedure or a scale of punishment. They are structureless and vague. This may be seen, for example, in the total lack of judicial procedure for the punishment of sorcery, a delict rated as highly antisocial and yet, aside from public scorn, punished only by Ialulep, the chief deity of the Ulithians, and by countersorcery by the intended victim. Nevertheless, supernatural sanctions are effective and as a consequence additionally inhibit the development of law. An intriguing use of sorcery is its employment by an individual against persons who defecate on his land. One might speculate on the extent to which the threat of contagious magic serves to promote sanitation in the atoll.

The structure of the law is as crudely developed as its concept. Codes are unclearly defined, procedures for the mediation of disputes are sporadic, and courts are absent.

Although code is weakly developed, it is not altogether negligible. There are brief reports in the literature, concerning this atoll and other islands in the area, of a principle of talion or equivalent retaliation in effect early in the century. They pertain to bodily injury. If a victim lost an arm or a hand, his relatives could inflict the same damage on the assailant. If he lost one or both eyes, they could inflict a like injury on the culprit.

But we cannot be sure if the principle of the *lex talionis* was always applied exactly. For example, in addition to retaliation against the person of the offender, there could be seizure of his house and other belongings. Moreover, a lesser offense, such as the tearing of an earlobe, was punished by payment of a ball of turmeric, no mention being made of the tearing of the earlobe of the offender. Evidence of code is seen in the penalty for loss of both legs, but here loss of land rather than equivalent retaliation was involved. It is said that a man who had mutilated the sex organs of another man would be put to death by the whole village, yet once more the details are lacking. There can be little doubt, however, that in the western Carolines there once did exist a code of indemnity of varying degrees of precision.

If, then, we display any indecision as to the strength of the Ulithian judicial code, it results from our difficulty in finding regularity. Law implies regularity, and regularity must be seen in litigation. Lacking litigation, even a hypothetical answer as to what constitutes the law cannot always be framed.

Numerous acts which in many societies would be considered delicts fail to qualify as involving the juridical for the simple reason that they are nonexistent. Thus, abortion and infanticide are not practiced, so any reaction to them can only be stated in hypothetical terms. Homicide, according to the oldest inhabitants, has never occurred within their memory, although, to be sure, in 1949 a demented youth found a loaded wartime carbine and killed two men with it. This is obviously a special situation in which no culpability was charged against the youth because of his acute psychosis. Sodomy, bestiality, and prostitution are unknown in the atoll and consequently, again, there has been no formation of juridical concepts and procedures regarding them.

As for the mediation of disputes, here again there is little regularity. The society does not exercise its authority or even its prestige in terminating litigation. Perhaps the area of most persistent and gnawing controversy pertains to land rights; grudges may be carried on covertly or even openly during the whole of men's lifetimes. Yet here there is no instrumentality to decide disputes one way or another and the complexity of the problem constantly increases. Some of the cause behind the lack of procedure obviously lies in the kinship character of sanctions. With kinsmen applying punishment in their customarily diffuse fashion against transgressors who are members of their group, process fails to receive encouragement for its development. Incest, adultry, thieving, lying, and quarrelling, for example, are essentially handled by the kinsmen of the offender, who may berate, beat, or otherwise punish him and—though this is inconsistent—seek to appease the kinsmen of the aggrieved party with gifts if they belong to another group.

It has been commented that courts are absent. They can be said to be present only in the sense that they are made up of the plaintiff and public opinion. Thus, where a plaintiff takes such action as the imposition of a distraint, without the intervention of a third party, the only tribunal is that of public opinion, which may recognize that the complaint of the aggrieved party is just, his procedure proper, and his assessment of damages reasonable. If the defendant feels the force of public opinion so strongly—as he usually does, for distraint is not exercised lightly—that he accepts the charges and makes compensation, then we may say that in a very loose sense there are courts in Ulithi. But this is perhaps going beyond the bounds. Actually, if we are to admit the presence of incipient courts at all it is in the deliberations of the men's councils; yet even here cases are adjudicated in a legal sense only by stretching the definition of the word legal.

The most fundamental aspect of law, which is to say the systematic and formal application of force by the state for the support of explicit rules of conduct, is as weakly represented as is concept and structure, for the use or threat of coercion is ordinarily neither impersonal nor delegated to parties acting on behalf of society. The cold neutrality of an impartial judge is nowhere to be found. Instead, the use or threat of physical force is mostly exercised by private parties acting in their own behalf. In such contexts, glimmerings of law in the stricter sense come from the tacit support given the aggrieved party against the actions of the defendant, these actions being diffusely felt as injurious to the general social interest.

Yet occasional exercise of a kind of sovereign, impersonal force must be conceded. As will be duly documented in the next section, the king wields the threat of force in certain matters infringing on him as the head of his miniature state. Allied to this is the authority exercised by the men's councils. The implication of force is vaguely felt behind their verbal chastisements of individuals who offend the community by such acts as shirking communal chores, disrupting the successful termination of a communal fishing effort by their thoughtless incursion into the area, defecating in unseemly public places, and ignoring prohibitions broadly referred to as *etap,* or taboos.

There can be no question but that the use of force is repugnant to Ulithians. The prevailing attitude is irenic—operating toward peace or conciliation.

While exile is apparently unknown nowadays, it seems to have existed in the past as a method of avoiding trouble rather than punishing one for making it. During his voyage around the world early in the last century, Kotzebue heard from his informant, Kadu, a man originally from Woleai but picked up by the Russians in the Marshalls, of an act of banishment intended to repress further delinquency. Kadu says that on the island of Mogmog in Ulithi the trees were regularly robbed of their best fruit, and when it was at long last discovered that the thief was a boy, they first merely scolded him, then tied him up at night and shut him up so he could not go on his depredations. But "the sly thief knew how to frustrate all these precautions, and continued as before." In despair, several persons rowed the young man to a remote, uninhabited island of the group, but the trees were robbed as before. The boy had used the trunk of a tree as a boat. They destroyed this and then enjoyed some respite. But once, when a party sought to discover how he was faring alone on the isle, they could not find him. As they searched, he stole their canoe and set out for the atoll of Sorol. Here he talked the chief of the atoll into sending a war party to Mogmog to seize and murder the chief and take the supreme power. But the people were frustrated on landing. "The instigator was punished by death. The people of Sorol returned uninjured to their island." The point Kotzebue tried to make is that everything was done to prevent misdeeds. The ultimate retribution was forced on the people. The example is interesting but does not answer many questions. Were the people who tied up the boy and later rowed him into exile acting on behalf of the village? Probably not. They could have been his kinsmen. Was exile a habitual practice?

In a letter written in 1722 while he was on Guam interviewing some castaways before his voyage to Ulithi, Father Cantova writes: "Criminals are not punished by either imprisonment or corporal punishment. It is enough to exile them to another island." Perhaps exile was a kind of sanction in those days, rather than a preventive. But again, who ordered the exile? Who executed the order?

Closely related to law, yet only quasi-legal, is the conventionalization of such diffuse sanctions as public contempt, criticism, and withdrawal. Here one does not find the systematic and impersonal application of force in the maintenance of individual rights and in the public interest. Nevertheless, the results are similar to those of law and act in its place. They have much the same effect as naked force.

Perhaps the best example of this is the bizarre exposure to ridicule offered through the *hamath* song, which bears the same name as the *hamath* dance. While the dance is connected with female puberty rites, it is seized upon as an occasion for redressing a grievance. The person who launches the procedure enlists the aid of his friends to compose and sing songs of derision and exposure while performing the dance, which, apart from its use in this context, is always frankly erotic or even lewd.

Let us say that a woman wishes to end her husband's philanderings with other women. She will secretly arrange with some women friends to make up a song to accompany the *hamath* dance. In this song reference may be made to the inadequacy of the man's sexual organ, to his clumsiness in his relations with women, or to his preference for eating chicken instead of catching fish—a mark of laziness. The man is humiliated and sets about trying to discover who initiated the *hamath* against him. He summons his men friends to retaliate in kind, whether or not the identity of his specific critic is known. If known, the men sing obscene words about the woman's easy virtue and deprecate her anatomy. If unknown, the men chant songs against women in general, taunting them as so sexually inadequate that the men must find solace with women on other islands. The next night, the women reply with new songs directed against the man. The contest continues sometimes for many days and may end when the women pick up stones and throw them at the men dancers. The original center of all this attention is usually chastened sufficiently for him to mend his ways. The effect goes even further than this; it may clear the air between men and women in general by allowing them to unburden themselves of pent-up grievances, and it may also serve to put all of them on the defensive lest as individuals they are exposed to the blasting words of the *hamath*.

Another conventionalization of criticism along lines that are quasi-legal is to be seen in the formalized song directed by a group of women against a member of their sex who shirks the performance of communal labor ordered by the men's council through the council of female elders. As the tardy offender approaches the cluster of women already at work, they initiate a lugubrious, slow chant naming the culprit and specifying her indolence. They keep repeating the chant until the guilty party has settled into the full swing of her duties. An air of merriment seems to pervade the gesture but there can be little doubt of its ultimate efficacy, at least for a time.

Leaves of Distraint

The most developed legal institution in Ulithi is indubitably the *harme-chung*, or distraint. It is an act designed to insure that an offender will make restitution for a wrong. Ideally, according to Anglo-Saxon common law, the distrainer takes the property of the wrongdoer into his own custody as a pledge that satisfaction will be forthcoming. In Ulithian practice, we may view the distraint as sometimes doing this, but sometimes acting without actual seizure of property. An act is performed with leaves to signify that the reputation and well-being of the offender, as it were, are now in the hands of the distrainer, who will redeem this reputation and well-being on payment of gift fines.

The word *harmechung* seems to be generic for "young leaves," but in actual practice the young leaves are always the young white ones of a growing coconut tree. These leaves, called *ubwoth,* always have highly ritualistic connotations, being used in magic and religion by specialists who wear them tied around the head, neck, arms, and ankles. They are also used by performers in either sacred or secular dances. The term *ubwoth* is often used as a synonym for the *harmechung.*

As an object, the *harmechung* are the leaves, fastened either to a stick planted in some appropriate place, often the locale of the transgression, or else tied directly to some property belonging to the offender. When it is thus displayed it means that a person has declared a sanction against another person.

The unusual feature of the distraint in Ulithi is that it is imposed unilaterally, without the benefit of a hearing or court, and yet has the support of the society. The assumption is that the distraint is not exercised frivolously, and that due reflection and adequate evidence have preceded the decision to resort to it. The object of the levy is expected to acknowledge his guilt, either implicitly or explicitly, and to atone for it by the payment of an indemnity or the forfeiture of property, which may be destroyed by the distrainer instead of being put to use.

Some hypothetical examples will bring out the multifaceted character of this legal institution.

The most serious application of the *harmechung* is in offenses against sovereignty or political authority. Such offenses may impinge on the king as the symbol of sovereignty, and include lese majesty. They may also encompass offenses against a village, whereby the council head initiates punitive action. Unwarranted intrusion into a territory is one of the most common occasions for resentment, and such trespass is regarded as an offense when it is committed by an outsider, either foreign to the atoll or to the district. For example, if a canoe from outside of Ulithi comes to the atoll and fails to report to the council house on Mogmog, that canoe will have leaves tied to one end of its hull as a sign that it has been confiscated for failure to observe the ritual. Should a canoe within the atoll arrive at another island in Ulithi and fail to perform the ritual, it too will be tied with young coconut leaves and be confiscated or even destroyed. Should a canoe pass through the area of one district on its way to another district without stopping to pay its respects, it again is subject to the penalty of the distraint. So is a canoe that has fished in grounds not belonging to its district.

It sometimes happens that an offending canoe cannot be seized. The act of *harmechung* cannot be performed literally but word will be sent to the lineage owning the canoe that it has been declared confiscated. The lineage must accept the decision.

Since sailing canoes are owned by lineages, the latter are culpable. It is possible to procure the return of a canoe that has been confiscated by making gift payments to the injured party, that is, either the king or a district chief. These payments are colorfully called "untying the young coconut leaves." It is no mere coincidence that canoes play so large a part in the law, for they are not only the instruments by which trespass is effected but constitute extremely valuable property as well.

The king also imposes the leaf sanction against any district that fails to send first fruits to Mogmog when certain kinds of plant foods are being gathered. He may also impose it for failure to contribute fish for a certain annual ritualistic feast given for the two leading chiefs of Mogmog.

The leaf sanction is seriously invoked when a district secretly kills a green turtle instead of sending it to Mogmog to be killed and distributed ritualistically. Green turtles have sacred connotations, and in any event are under the control of the island of Mogmog, which is to say, the two district chiefs there. It happened that for some years the turtle ritual had not been performed. The reasons for this are highly involved but go back ultimately to the suspension of the pagan ritual investing the king. The island of Fassarai, knowing the ritualistic killing of sea turtles had not been perpetuated, killed some of the huge reptiles clandestinely. The chiefs of Mogmog, one of whom was the king, sent word of a distraint to Fassarai, forbidding anyone at all from that island to carry on any kind of fishing whatsoever. Since fish is the most prized of foods, this was a severe blow. After two or three months of deprivation, the people of Fassarai brought an "untying" to the offended chiefs. It consisted of garments, dried leaves to make into sails, turmeric, rope, cloth, and hawksbill carapaces (not taboo). The two chiefs on Mogmog accepted the indemnity and shared it with each of the two council chiefs on the island. As is customary, although the payments were nominally made to them, they distributed the goods to all the people. An apology had to accompany Fassarai's indemnity.

The island of Mogmog holds a privileged position in the *harmechung* system by virtue of its being the seat of sovereignty. In a dispute with another island, it may distrain but not be distrained against. However, in civil cases involving challenges against Mogmog lineages, this immunity does not apply.

Behind the leaf sanction is the threat of force, and it is here that the main ingredient of law manifests itself. It is not necessary to use force against the chief of an offending island, since he would not think of ignoring a *harmechung*. Tradition and public opinion are too strong for that. However, in private cases an individual may choose to defy the imposition of a leaf sanction. Should he do so, his own village would punish him by damaging his house or canoe, if he has one, and confiscate any movable property. It should be pointed out that such action is not taken in ordinary civil cases but only when the individual has been the object of a leaf sanction imposed by his lineage or some chief.

Recourse to distraint in civil cases, as opposed to public or criminal types, seems predominantly to involve disputes between lineages rather than individuals, even though the lineages are represented in the dispute by their chiefs. A typical litigation might involve the payment of *momwoi*. This payment is a kind of compensation made after a divorce to one's former spouse if one is the first to remarry after the termination of the marriage. In a way, the payment signalizes the complete divorce, for prior to that a couple is actually only separated. It does not serve as acknowledgment of guilt in the dispute that led to the breakup. In actuality, the payment is made by one lineage to another. Should a lineage fail to make payment of the *momwoi*, it becomes the recipient of distraint. If its delinquent member is a woman, the land she has brought into the marriage is distrained by tying young coconut leaves to a stick, which is then implanted on the land in question. Her ex-husband keeps the land. If the offender is the man, his land may not be distrained. Instead, verbal distraint is declared by her lineage against all of his property in movables: rope, pots, knives, pigs, chicken, and so on. So obvious to all is the failure for an ex-spouse, man or woman, to pay the *momwoi* that the objects of the distraint make no retaliation. Their guilt is acknowledged by their silent yielding to the seizure.

The leaf sanction is obviously an effective institution in preventing the indefinite extension of conflict. While it substitutes for physical force, the ultimate recourse to physical coercion is implied. Being recognized by the society as a just and valid procedure it brings finality into a dispute, so preventing deterioration into a feud. The leaf sanction is indubitably at a higher level of the juridical than is most rudimentary law in the atoll.

Liability

Ulithians make full and reasonable allowance for deviations resulting from lack of comprehension between what is right and what is wrong. Even though many violations of the legal norms can be attributed to the feebleminded or insane, it is considered that those individuals who are mentally incompetent should not be held responsible for their acts. While on the atoll, I was deeply impressed by the solicitude with which the people treated a young manic who damaged property, refused to work, struck his father, pursued women threateningly, and menaced small children with fishing spears. They tolerated an old woman who was accustomed to steal, spread falsehoods, hoard food, and shirk communal chores. These psychotics were shown every consideration and sympathy. Effort was made to draw them and others like them into the pattern of daily life.

Children are often held unresponsible for their acts, their culpability depending on their age and the nature of the offense. Children who offend within the family are held responsible to the family but not beyond that. Those who transgress against a neighbor and are of an age sufficiently advanced to know they have done wrong, must have have their parents compensate the injured party with some item of goods. If the child is too young to have realized his culpability, the family may extend a gift to the injured party in order to demonstrate its regret.

Involuntary or unwitting transgressions do not incur liability. Should a man accidentally damage a canoe belonging to someone else, or unintentionally break a borrowed knife, or injure a bystander while lifting a heavy object to his shoulders, he is considered blameless. Indeed, the injured party may be considered to be the victim of a spirit or other supernatural power that has simply used the offender as an instrument for performing the damage or injury.

The owners of animals that inflict damage, bite, steal food, or commit a nuisance in a man's house or garden may be liable for the act if it is due to negligence in controlling the animal, usually a dog or a pig. But if the damage or injury can be traced to such actions on the part of the injured party as teasing the animal or unleashing it when tied, then the owner is not liable. If a third party has teased or unleased the animal, he is the one who is responsible.

Rank as such conveys no immunity for violation of the law. If anything, a chief or other person of high status is held especially culpable in any transgression, as he should serve as a model of comportment. However, there is no evidence that this ideal is given expression in practice. There is no doubt, however, that the force of public opinion is such that it serves to exact of its chiefs a spirit of *noblesse oblige.*

5

The Transcendental World

I T IS NOT POSSIBLE to characterize Ulithian religion in holistic terms, for it is overwhelmingly eclectic. It is as if the people, having been exposed throughout centuries to myriads of other people's adjustments to the supernatural, have incorporated anything in their armamentarium that suggests the possibility of reward. No haughty disdain of alien creeds or rituals, no smug satisfaction with indigenous creations marks the Ulithian attitude towards the transcendental. Consequently, side by side with ancestor worship is a belief in a pantheon of celestial and terrestrial gods, an involvement with animistic spirits, a concern with the other world of punishment and reward, a recourse to mediums, a reliance on magic and divination, and a guide to things taboo.

Included in this conglomerate is a belief in totemic beings; but totemism has not caught much hold in the atoll because it belongs to the alien clans that have established precarious residence there, and in any event is more social than religious in character.

Ancestors Who Care

Father Cantova, a remarkably reliable informant, wrote in 1722 about Carolinian religion and tells us enough about the worship of ancestors to reassure us that the practice has endured long and without much change. The ensuing account, however, is not drawn from him and refers specifically to Ulithi.

At the basis of the system of ancestor worship is a recognition that some spirit beings have an originally human origin rather than the impersonal one of the spirits of nature.

Ancestors are of course people and consequently are possessed of souls. The soul of the living person is lodged in the head, and ingress and egress take place where the bregmatic fontanelle of infancy is located. This unossified membranous interval in the frontal portion of the cranium is the spot where the soul enters the baby at birth. The soul is not a prisoner; it may, especially in dreams and illness, leave the body and wander or fly about and then return. When a person dies the soul leaves forever and is then called a ghost. Ghosts hover in the vicinity of their graves for four days after death and subsequently fly away to the island of Angaur in the west, where they bathe. They then proceed to make their way upward through various levels to the Sky World, where a decision is made by the chief deity there as to their fate. The ghosts of the dead do not lose interest in the living; in fact, they are an extension of society because of the interest they take in human activities.

Of the vast pool of departed ancestors, most are soon forgotten by the living, while others achieve varying degrees of prominence and remembrance. Since ordinary ghosts are of little practical consequence and quickly achieve the oblivion that is the destiny of the undistinguished, they may be immediately dismissed.

The ghosts that are remembered are of various kinds, but all have a link with lineages. A lineage ghost is one who has returned from the Sky World to possess a lineage mate. Of course, such a spirit is known by name and gains a certain amount of ritualistic attention and respect. But if in the course of his or her necromantic career he begins to falter in the performance of the services expected of him, he becomes neglected and ultimately forgotten. His memory to be sure is not as transient as that of a new ghost who has failed completely to make his presence known through a medium; on the other hand, it endures so briefly that after the passage of a few generations his lineage cannot recall his name.

A more important type of lineage ghost is one who has made so great a contribution to members of his lineage that he is elevated to the uppermost position for that kin group. In the course of his ascendancy he supplants the extant number one ghost, who is thereby demoted and relegated in the course of time to oblivion. Oddly enough, this exalted type of spirit is known as a "little ghost," but only by comparison with two individual ghosts of wide renown who will be examined later. All lineages, except very minor ones, possess a little ghost and provide a shrine for him, located in the house of the head of the lineage. The shrine consists essentially of a bamboo grid from which are suspended offerings of coconut oil, leis, loincloths, and turmeric. The oil is left there indefinitely and the leis until they have withered, but the loincloths and turmeric are removed after about ten to twenty days and given to members of the household to use. Neither of these may be employed in connection with a corpse or a funeral. There is a pragmatic tone to the arrangement. The offerings are essentially payments for services performed. Usually, no offering is left for a ghost until he has made an appearance; however, on occasion a family will present offerings in anticipation of a visit, discontinuing the offerings should the ghost fail to manifest himself through a medium. The principal gainer seems to be the custodian of the shrine, who is normally the eldest male member of the lineage but may come from the patrilineal side of the little ghost. He is the only one who may receive the offerings and look after the shrine. He may or may not be the ghost's medium. In any event, many of the offerings ultimately come into his hands.

Lineages may on occasion adopt a little ghost from another lineage on the grounds that they do not have a successful one of their own. The intrusive clans on Ulithi have similarly borrowed the services of little ghosts. Thus, through borrowing as well as replacement there is some fluidity in the system, yet as documentary evidence has shown change is not characteristic. The mobility of the system is rather a sign of the great democracy prevailing in the atoll, for anyone's ghost may achieve a position of eminence, eminence depending not on one's rank while alive but on accomplishment after death. In his lifetime a little ghost may have been a chief or an ordinary man, a female as well as a male, an infant as well as an adult.

In ancestor worship, the medium plays an important role, for it is through him that the ancestors provide the kind of information sought by the living in the conduct of their lives. The medium is the means by which advice, warnings, and facts are transmitted. While in a state of possession he trembles a good deal and on occasion may go into an epilepticlike fit. He utters the words of the spirit in clear and intelligible language, rather than strange verbiage or incomprehensible mutterings. The information imparted in trance communication pertains to the things that most concern the Ulithian: the feasibility of an ocean voyage, the safety of relatives away from home, the cause of an illness, the attitude of a loved one, the approach of a typhoon, and the like. The experience of having been possessed by the dead is a trying one. When the ghost leaves, the mouthpiece emerges from his trance and is given water and a massage. He recovers from his feeling of malaise but has no recollection of his experience and cannot repeat what the spirit said during that time. The seance is not on this account wasted, for the medium's relatives have been listening attentively to all that has been said.

One might suppose that attaining the rank of principal ghost of a lineage would be the pinnacle of success for an ancestral spirit, but there is a status beyond that. There exists a social class of lineage ghosts called "great ghosts," of which there are only two in number. Ulithians are adamant as to their historicity and do not confuse them with spirits of high eminence who are not thought of as having once been mortals. True, these ghosts have reached such heights that they have journeyed a long way on the road to apotheosis, and their fame has spread throughout a vast area of the Carolines. Nevertheless, they have human origins. This is hard to verify for the great ghost called Iongolap. It is easier to document for the other, named Marespa.

Early mention is made of Iongolap in the literature. The Russian explorer Kotzebue was told by Kadu in 1817 of his great importance at that time not only in Ulithi but Yap, Ngulu, and Fais as well. The information is scanty but discloses to us that the god "visits distant islands where he is acknowledged," and that several "temples," where offerings are made, are built for him at Ulithi, Yap, and Ngulu.

Iongolap, according to Ulithian informants and mythology, was born in the atoll a long time ago of a woman who had left her home on Yap in anger because of a quarrel, and had created the islands of Ulithi by strewing sand on the surface of the sea. Iongolap's father was a Yapese, and when the boy left

Ulithi to visit him on Yap, his father gave him most of the islands of the Carolinian archipelago, and some others besides. One day Iongolap wanted to leave Yap to visit his mother on Ulithi but the people would not let him go. Instead, they sent some men to the atoll, instructing them to bring back gifts to present to Iongolap. That is why, it is said, Ulithi continues sending religious tribute to Yap even today. But occasionally Iongolap does visit his birthplace, joining the crews of the Ulithian canoes as they return home after paying tribute to Yap. Statements in the literature indicate that when he is at the atoll he "lives" at the house of the Fasilus lineage, the head lineage of the atoll and the one that supplies the paramount chief. These statements also assert that early in the present century a grandson of Iongolap lived in that same house. At any rate, despite the fact that the Yapese claim the ghost-become-god as their own, the people of Ulithi have other ideas and once a year hold a feast in his honor, with all islands of the atoll participating. He is turned to in time of need, especially when famine threatens. Obviously, notwithstanding the changes introduced by the process of myth making, the people of Ulithi consider Iongolap to be an ancestral ghost. Though we hear nothing regarding his necromantic accomplishments, the tacit assumption is that as a great ghost he surely must have reached such status because of his talent in providing information, presumably at first to members of the Fasilus lineage, later to the people of the whole atoll.

But the process of apotheosis has proceeded so far, as long ago as 1817, that it is hard to recognize in him a mere ancestor. Iongolap is the stuff of which gods are made. In one myth he sends a bird from Yap to Ulithi to look after his sister. The bird gives birth to a girl, who lives with this sister until they have a serious quarrel over food. Iongolap's sister deserts the girl and returns to Yap, but the girl gives birth to a son—grandchild of the bird. The son lives in the heavens but returns each day to earth to do the cooking. One day he went to Yap in a canoe that had been transformed by magic from a stone, and the stone canoe may still be seen in a channel there. This myth, collected in 1909 by a German anthropologist, is supplemented by another in which Iongolap sends a spirit to a man on Ulithi to teach him how to make a fishhook and to fish with it. Another myth, this time from Yap, has Ionglap born there near a village in the district of Gagil, which it will be recalled is the overlord of Ulithi and the islands further to the east. These myths explain not only why a series of complex festivals are held on Yap throughout the year in honor of the deity but also why he has a relationship to Ulithi that is expressed through political subordination and various rituals.

In the course of time a new great ghost named Marespa appeared on the scene. He is completely Ulithian and has largely supplanted his predecessor. Regarding his historicity there is little or no doubt. I have gathered his genealogy and certain anecdotal materials that not only authenticate his existence but help us place his date of birth at about 1868. Like Iongolap, he is said by Ulithians to belong to the dominant Fasilus lineage. His birthplace is the island of Lam, and his grave on that island still stands.

Marespa died when he was only a few weeks or months old. Soon afterwards he possessed one of his relatives and continued to use him for a time as his mouthpiece. Speaking in the high-pitched voice of a baby, he communicated forthcoming events, it is said, with such startling accuracy that his fame soon spread throughout the atoll. But it did not stop at the verges of Ulithi; it jumped rapidly to Yap, where, in Gagil district, he became second only to Iongolap in importance. In view of the fact that Gagil considers Ulithians to be low caste people, this concession to their great ghost attests to the eagerness with which people of the Carolines seize upon any supernatural phenomenon that has promise of success.

It did not take long for Marespa's fame to spread further afield. He became the leading ghost of the eastward islands called the Woleai. Undoubtedly, the receptivity he encountered was partly inspired by the superordinate position of Ulithi with respect to these islands in the Gagil domain, but it is likely that his great talents as a ghost were even more persuasive. To the west, he caught the fancy of Palau, where it is said that one lineage, possibly originally from Ulithi, asked for and received permission from the atoll to build a shrine for him, just as the people of Ulithi and the Woleai had already done. Beyond Palau, at the westernmost limits of Micronesia, the islands of Sonsorol, Pulo Anna, Merir, and Tobi are reputed to have found a place for him despite their recognition of a certain local ghost as the most powerful of all. Ngulu, a satellite of Yap outside the Gagil sphere and closely allied to Ulithi by virtue of certain common historical, cultural, and linguistic relations, is said to have adopted Marespa as its chief ghost. In all these islands, he became so identified with the people that they built their own local shrines for him and did not take offerings for him to Ulithi. It is possible that the facts about Marespa have been exaggerated in Ulithi's favor by local informants and that the places in the extensive area to which his fame and activity traveled may be only those where Ulithians have been present as immigrants or visitors, but there can be no doubt of his importance. A Polish anthropologist recorded some details in the last century concerning his presence in Palau, and a German anthropologist provides fuller information garnered in 1909 on Ngulu atoll. In 1947 an American anthropologist working on the atoll of Ifaluk collected some songs in which the ghost is several times mentioned.

With such talent in predicting typhoons, warning of impending epidemics, revealing the loss of voyagers at sea, describing events in distant places, forecasting the arrival of schools of fish, and other choice morsels of information so dearly sought by anxious people, Marespa was destined to go beyond the status of a great ghost. Like Iongolap before him, he began to have woven about him a tissue of mythology that set in motion the metamorphosis towards godhood. Then suddenly his progress was halted by the encroachments of alien creeds and administrations, and he lost his position of pre-eminence where previously he had been shown honor and deference. But on Ulithi there are those who still remember his halcyon days of glory.

Little has been said here of the role of the dead in participating in human affairs. Like solicitous parents they provide blessing and protection, but at the same time are not averse to inflicting ghostly retribution against transgressors of the moral order. Such parental-like involvement makes them, in a sense,

active members of society. For they are never very far from the dreary intercourse of daily life.

Ancestor worship is not a unique local phenomenon. Despite inadequate
reporting, it is obvious that throughout Micronesia all the conventional criteria
of ancestor worship are met: the historicity of the ghosts of ancestors, the trans-
ference to them of an attitude of reverence, and the employment of ritualistic
practices designed to effect interaction between the living and the dead. Nor is
the apotheosis experienced by Iongolap and Marespa unknown elsewhere. Similar
instances have been noted, for example, in the Gilbert Islands, and it is likely
that the process of deification of mortals was once not uncommon in all of Micronesia. Ancestor worship fits the prevailing culture, with its strong emphasis
on kinship, and is consistent with the highly personal character of social relations.

Demons Who Menace

Ulithians take cognizance also of superhuman beings who lack human
origins. The generic name for such beings is *ialus,* which may be translated as
"spirit." They range from lowly to lofty.

The less elevated of these spirits live in close intimacy with mortals and
lack the dignity of gods. They are not the object of a cult. Some are benevolent
but most are malevolent, and in any event demand attention and respect, even
though they do not merit worship. For want of a better word they may be referred to as demons.

Demons are reported in vague and conflicting ways by the natives. Some
say they have one large eye, others say two, and still others say four. They are
variously depicted as anthropomorphic or balls of fire, male or female, clothed
or nude, and transparent or nontransparent. Some say they are black, whereas
others depict them as brown, blue, or white. Demons have been observed sitting, standing, walking, swimming, or suspended in air a few inches off the
ground. Some have pursued people and even wrestled with them. They have
been heard to moan, whistle, sing, and talk. They have been seen in various
haunts—houses, groves, beaches, and the sea. They have been observed during
the daytime and at night.

For the most part demons are anonymous. They are classified in four
main categories, depending on whether their habitat is a tree, a burial plot, the
earth, or the sea. People do not ordinarily think of them as being male or female. They are well aware of the demons' sinister attitude toward human beings
and are quick to attribute illness, misfortune, and strange happenings to them.
Ialus of this type threaten men constantly and force them to maintain a constant
vigil against them. So they are not simple pranksters; rather, they are the source
of much of the misery afflicting mankind.

Some demons are known by name and their personal traits. One, a tree
spirit, causes blindness, stomach pains, and a sickness that enormously distends

the abdomen. Another tree spirit is responsible for gonorrhea. Another demon, who lives in the coral holes of the sea surrounding the island of Lam, has a bad reputation and is greatly feared, yet no one knows what causes him to be angered, or can say if he has in fact ever injured anyone. A curious spirit, whose name is greeted with laughter even though he is feared, is held in low esteem by the people because he employs an absurd method of catching fish and lobsters. He uses his penis as a light to attract these sea fauna in the dark. He has been seen walking at night along the reef and on the surface of the water. On account of the delicate nature of his fishing technique one refrains from mentioning him by name in mixed company; instead, a euphemism, "the spirit that uses a torch," must be employed. Finally, although the list of named demons is not exhausted, there is a female spirit who has jurisdiction over the sacred swamp gardens. These are sacred to the extent that many taboos must be observed by persons with respect to entering these gardens. Not permitted to enter are: people who have eaten or defecated during the day; people who are in mourning for a close relative, or have washed a corpse, or dug a grave in the past five months; women who are menstruating; women who are barren; persons who have had sexual relations during the previous six days; men who have fished with a line during the previous four days; fish magicians who have used a certain type of hook during the five previous lunar months; and, lastly, medical practitioners who are currently engaged in treating a patient. This demon, whose hair and skin are reputed to be gray in color, always carries a basket. Her very appearance frightens people, even when they are innocent of any wrongdoing. She lives in all four of the swamp gardens, and if she feels that their sanctity has been violated she punishes the offenders by inflicting on them such diseases as yaws, filariasis, and small boils, as well as other maladies. Her anger may be expressed in a broader way by sending insects to attack the plants growing in the gardens, causing them to die. It is plain that the great concern which the natives have with the food supply is reflected in the numerous precautions they must take to see that nothing will endanger the productivity of the gardens.

Named or not, then, demons cause many of the tribulations that humans must face, and this includes insanity, too. They cannot be won over through prayer but fortunately they can sometimes be coaxed or bribed with gifts and sweet talk. Certainly they serve a positive role in causing the community to maintain proper concern with certain aspects of daily living. In any event they help explain away perplexing phenomena not otherwise explicable, and in doing so lift the gnawing worry that comes from the uncertainty of not knowing the source of one's woes.

A special kind of demon is the ogre. Spirits of this genre eat human beings but they are so outlandishly stupid that ultimately they get their comeuppance from a mortal of greater guile and courage than they possess. Ogres play no part in the religious system, being found principally in the folklore. In a way one must feel a certain compassion towards their fumbling efforts to fill their stomachs with human victims. Though they may terrorize the land, they are fated to end ignominiously, sometimes at the hands of a boy or even a madman.

Gods Who Control

In less intimate contact than either the ancestral dead or the demons infesting every nook and cranny of man's habitat are the gods of sky and earth. True, they are awesome and powerful, yet they are not always concerned with daily life and are not the object of as dynamic a religious cult as are the spirits of the dead. Their worship and propitiation proceeds in irregular fashion.

The gods play no part in the creation of the world. Myths do not tell us how the world originated; at best they tell only how particular islands were formed. In doing so they presuppose the existence of the world and certain supernaturals within it. The lack of cosmogonic myths may be no more than the effects of cultural erosion, for other islands of the Carolines sometimes have accounts telling of the creation of the world, trees, grass, people, and so on.

The pantheon is bifurcated into gods whose realm is the Sky World and those who dwell on earth. The former are more involved with the after-life of mortals, the latter with the present life and its instrumentalities. There is no important distinction in their nature and both branches come under the rubric of *ialus*. They are not affiliated with kin groups; instead, they belong to all the society.

A better appreciation of the spirits of the sky can be gained by looking first at the structure and features of their domain. The Sky World, called Lang (*cf.* Hawaiian Lani) is conceived of as constituted of four levels, the fourth being the one where the great deities live. Each plane has distinctive features and, although these are fairly well delineated in the mythology of other Carolinians, they are, except for the top level, vaguely known to Ulithians. Souls on the way to their final destinations must traverse these levels.

In the highest level of Lang there is an enormous house where the chief deities of the sky branch of the pantheon live. To it come all the fresh spirits of the dead in order to be judged by Ialulep, the greatest *ialus* of them all. For a figure of such pre-eminence strangely little is known about his personality and experiences. He is said never to bother to come down to earth, as do other celestial spirits on occasion. His main role is to listen to the newly arrived spirits as they are being interrogated at the great house by his son, Lugeilang. He listens and decides the fate of each spirit.

Ialulep, which means Great Spirit, is known elsewhere in the Carolines and is generally portrayed as of enormous size and tremendous age. His hair is white. So old and weak is he that men must help him to open his mouth and keep his upper lip from hanging down too far when he wishes to eat. His eyelids are so heavy that when he wishes to look over the world two men have to lift his eyelids. When the door of his house slams there is thunder on earth. In some places, he is believed to control life itself. In his hands he holds the thread of life of each human being, and when he decides that a man is to die he utters words to that effect and tears the thread extending to the brain of the person in question.

Much more is known on Ulithi about Lugeilang, his son. He is a colorful god who used to be in the habit of maintaining trysts on earth, where once he met a woman who subsequently gave birth to their son, the famous trickster god of the Carolines known as Iolofath.

Iolofath is perhaps the best known of all the characters of Carolinian mythology. He has many of the traits of the Polynesian Maui: brashness, craftiness, precocity, mischievousness, and lustiness. A Ulithian version of the Iolofath cycle has it that he was born when his mother, mistress of Lugeilang, tugged on a lock of her hair and he issued forth from her head, with all his teeth erupted, and able to walk and talk. Against his father's wishes he ascends to the Sky World on a cloud of smoke to visit him. At each of the four levels of Lang he has experiences that provoke him into performing mischievous deeds. Thus, at the first level he sees several boys playing with a scorpion fish. Annoyed because they will not let him into their circle, he causes the fish to develop spines which prick the boys' fingers and make them cry. At the second level he is again rebuffed by some boys playing with a shark. He causes the fish to develop teeth and bite the boys. Their parents beat him and he flees to the third level, where several boys are playing with a sting ray that is without stingers. He causes stingers to appear and jab the boys, for they too have rejected him as a playmate. Reaching the fourth level he finds men fetching timber to build the great house of the Sky World known as the Farmal. They are all fish but have human attributes, gliding back and forth, imperceptible in their appearance between the piscatory and the anthropomorphic.

The people of the fourth level are digging a hole into which to plant the great housepost of the Farmal. On seeing Iolofath they decide to kill him because he is a stranger. They induce him to go into the posthole and then they ram the post down on him. Red and green fluids squirt upwards and the people think this is his blood and bile, but he has tricked them by taking refuge in a pocket he has dug to the side of the hole. The fluids are merely red earth and green mountain apple leaves that he has put in his mouth. Our ingenious hero escapes from his subterranean prison by having termites eat a hole upward through the great housepost. He has ants bring him small morsels of coconut meat and an arum, and magically causes these to attain full size. He increases the size of a grain of sand until it becomes a rock. Dashing the coconut against the rock he cries out *"Soro!"* to the workmen below. They are astounded and immediately realize he is the son of Lugeilang. Thenceforth they treat him with deference.

The following day the young trickster goes from house to house distributing certain turtle meat. At the home of the procupine fish he scolds him for having spines. He next scolds the cornet fish because his head has no flesh; then the swellfish for having a big belly. When he arrives at the home of the halfbeak he does not find him in and so proceeds to make love to his wife. The halfbeak returns, catches the pair in the act, and kills Iolofath. It takes the efforts of his father, Lugeilang, to bring him back to life.

Another major theme in this myth cycle deals with the conflict between the trickster and his half-brother, whose mother is the true wife of Lugeilang and not a mortal mistress. No love is lost between the two brothers. In a cruel episode Iolofath kills his brother by severing his head but is persuaded by his father to put it back on. Later, this brother puts the trickster in his place by teaching him a lesson in magic.

In later episodes of the cycle, the trickster has mellowed considerably, and in a major episode acts as conciliator between a youth and the wife he has spurned.

Iolofath is not a god in the conventional sense. He mediates between the worlds celestial and terrestrial. After all, he is half-mortal and his behavior has many of the frailties of earthlings, which is probably what endears him to the natives. But still, he is one of the three principal figures in the Sky World and should not be looked upon simply as an unusual mortal. Although in some islands of the Carolines he imparts fire to mankind and decrees that men shall be mortal, he is neither a creator nor culture hero in Ulithi.

Other celestial figures are trivial in importance, acting principally as supporting actors in the myths of the three great gods.

Parallel to the celestial gods is a branch of the pantheon made up of deities of closer relationship to the people than are those in Lang. These gods enter more intimately into the lives of humans, who are keenly aware of their presence and influence. Chief among them are several deities connected with navigation and the sea.

Many of the terrestrial gods, who are far more numerous than the ones in heaven, are characters in a strange myth in which their progenitor exiles himself and his family from the Sky World where they originally lived and takes up permanent abode on earth. In making the transition they forsake their former names and adopt the names of gods in the world they have just deserted. Henceforth, they are identified only by their assumed names.

The father of the brood is Palulap, or Great Navigator. He is said to have brought knowledge of navigation and canoe building to mankind. However, the patron gods of these arts are two of his six sons. Some credit him also with teaching men the art of palm-leaf-knot divination, a practice of utmost importance not only in Ulithi but the rest of the Carolines as well.

His youngest son is Ialulwe, who, because he was born on earth, has a name of his own rather than a borrowed one. He is in practice the deity closest to the people of the atoll. He is the patron of navigators—men of great consequence in the society. Ialulwe is feared because of the punishment he metes out to violators of the mores of the society, and in this respect rivals any of the ancestral ghosts. But his attitude is generally a benevolent one. Of the two cabins constructed on the large seagoing canoes, one is devoted principally to him. In this little cabin, located over the booms of the outrigger, are placed offerings of turmeric, oil, carapaces, mats, and belts. Also included are an effigy of the god himself with two or more stingray stingers as legs. The effigy is used to fight off any sorcery that may possibly be directed against the navigator and his crew. Amulets and other objects of magical character are also placed in the cabin. The mixed nature of Ulithian supernaturalism is reflected in the intermingling in one place of religious and magical objects.

The other cabin, located on the leeward side of the canoe, is secular in nature, being used to store food and supplies, yet some objects of the same kind left for ancestral ghosts at their shrine are put in the cabin. It is not clear if some appeal to the ancestors is thereby intended; at any rate, no connection with Ialulwe is made.

Ialulwe has more than two eyes. Some say he has eyes all over his head, others say he has four eyes in all. There is always at least one eye at the back of his head, as his effigies reveal, this having to do with navigational techniques.

There is something undefinably strange about this god. He gains his knowledge of navigation while still being carried in his mother's womb. This he does while his father is instructing the other sons, of whom there are five. By the time he is born he is already a grown boy with a strong mind of his own and capable of unusual deeds. He is a loner who creates an island out of sand and then lives henceforth on it. When one of his brothers is wrecked at sea and attempts to crawl wearily on the island, he rebuffs and even blinds him because of his insubordination and the violation of certain maritime taboos. Yet while the brother is still in his blindness Ialulwe teaches him the art of navigation. The brother eventually returns to his family, after which he experiences the castigation of his own people because they do not recognize him as he sits at the beach, and are impatient with his gloomy forecasts concerning the suitability of the weather for an ocean voyage they are planning. Despite his warnings they make the trip, and all aboard, including his father, sister, and three of his brothers, perish. The myth that recounts these adventures gives expression to many of the ritual prohibitions of the sea observed in Ulithi.

A brother, also of patronlike character, is Solang, who dwells in canoes and is prayed to by canoe builders to enlist his help in making a good craft. Canoe building is an important and prestigeful art, surrounded by many prescriptions and taboos. Solang insists that none of his carpenters work late in the afternoon. Men who fail to heed this rule run the risk of intervention, as a result of which they mishandle their adzes and cut themselves. Solang permits no one to build a house or repair one on any island where the building or repairing of a canoe is already in progress. Violators, who run the risk of death, are simultaneously threatened from another quarter by the house deity, Thuchera, who has a parallel resentment against such dual activity. This god is the patron of house carpenters. He is not a member of the family to which Ialulwe and Solang belong.

The completing of a canoe is an important occasion, and the owners present gifts to Solang. These, consisting of such goods as turmeric and loincloths, are placed in the canoe and a prayer is uttered for the success and sturdiness of the vessel. In actual practice, the gifts come into the hands of the canoe builder, who turns them over to the master who taught him his art. Should his teacher be dead he keeps them for himself.

There are other terrestrial deities, but of lesser importance. Some of them are the remainder of Palulop's children, as well as his wife, but none of them seem to figure outside of mythology except the only daughter in the family, Ligafas. Like the other members of the family she has a connection with the sea. Her part in dooming the canoe in which members of her family were traveling serves to remind people that it is strictly taboo for a menstruating woman to undertake a sea voyage.

The only other terrestrial deity worth mentioning is Solal, not to be confused with Solang. He is merely referred to as lord of the nether regions, yet information from other islands of the Carolines suggest that he is coequal with the great celestial god, Ialulep. Apparently his high status has not been perpetuated in Ulithi. Nevertheless, he is the patron of the public fish magicians of the atoll, who pray to him to gain success in their complex and hazardous annual ritual to create an abundance of fish for the people. They do this just before they begin to drag their magical medicine bundles through the waters of Rowaryu channel.

Rituals That Tap
Supernatural Power

U LITHIANS DO NOT RELY solely on their complex of souls, ghosts, and gods to resolve their relationship to supernatural power. In addition, they envisage an essentially technological approach which uses ritual itself as the agent for the accomplishment of ends not achievable through the ordinary world of experience. The key to power rests not in the spirits but the rite.

At first glance it may seem a contradiction to discover that spirit beings are involved in much of this kind of ritual. They are often appealed to obsequiously. According to myths, they may even be the authors of the rites, teaching them to mankind. The problem is resolved, however, if one bears in mind that if the spirits are invoked it is not because they are expected to grant the desired end; rather, it is in order to receive their blessing and encouragement. The verbal portion of the rite is to be seen, then, not as a prayer petitioning the spirits to take action but as a means for accomplishing a desired result in its own right. Whatever partakes of the nature of prayer in the incantation is prefatory or ancillary to the main drive for results.

Many of the rites make no such allusion to spirit beings. The natives do not distinguish conceptually or terminologically between those that do and those that do not. They gather all these techniques under a single rubric that distinguishes them from prayers to ancestors and deities. This rubric is equivalent to our word "magic."

The ends for which magical techniques are a means are more egocentric than those of religion. Magic has less effect in supporting the moral order than in satisfying an immediate specific objective on the part of the magician himself, his client, or the society he may be called upon to serve. The magician is little concerned with the ethical system as such. If he observes taboos it is because they are regulations necessary for the success of his effort and not because they are requisite for a good life. To abstain from the use of certain wood to build a

61

fire, to prevent people from touching his person, to sleep apart from his wife— these have nothing to do with what is morally right in social behavior but what is expedient for the success of his ritual. Violating the compulsive rules of his art has little to do with incurring the disfavor of the gods; it is relevant mostly to the extent that it renders his efforts ineffective.

This might seem to imply that there is some speculation over the source of power. Such is not the case. Just as the power with which the spirits are endowed is taken for granted, so is the abstract force that the magical rite is intended to draw upon. People do not inquire into their nature. This simple acceptance of supernatural forces contrasts conspicuously with the complex proliferation of spirits and the elaboration of magical procedures.

Traits of the Rituals

The magic is not elaborate, requiring ordinarily the activity of but a single person. Even in the rituals of the fish and wave magicians, the assistants to these men take no hand in carrying out the techniques of the ritual. The assistants to the fish magicians paddle the canoe and fish; those who help the wave magicians hold on to a rope fastened around the waist of the performer so that he will not be dragged into the sea as he does his work at the shoreline. Their actions do not constitute part of the magic. Even where assistants are required to observe various taboos, it is only so they will not spoil the work of the magician, who must keep himself and his ritual free of contamination.

The magic never involves interaction with a responding audience. While spectators may look on, they are not encouraged to do so. In certain kinds of ritual the client may be on hand merely as an interested party.

The simplicity of Ulithian magic is also seen in the brevity of its duration. Most magic is performed in a matter of minutes or a portion of an hour, and is not repeated over and over. The longest ritual is that of the fish magician, who carries on his efforts for one to two months, but this is an exceptional length of time.

An examination of the techniques of magic reveals still further the simplicity with which they are endowed. Verbal symbols in the form of threats, powerful words, and imagery constitute the principal technique. There is a pleasing use of alliteration and a dramatic use of intonation. The language employed is often strongly garbled and archaic, so that it may be partially or completely unintelligible. What has been called the "coefficient of weirdness" in magical spells is high, and many of the persons who have memorized and used a spell are unable to translate or understand it. Yet most incantations are brief, and so, despite their quality of strangeness, they are not hard to memorize.

Next to linguistic symbols, the most important element in the magical techniques is the use of bodily ornaments. Strictly speaking, these objects are not really ornaments at all, and if they embellish, this is incidental to their true significance. Ritualistic ornaments are not instrumental in themselves, having no power without the incantations recited over them. Made of coral, plants, and other materials, they assume their dynamics through the spells spoken over them. An exception is the *ubwoth,* or young coconut leaf, referred to previously in connection with the placing of a distress against an accused party. Such young leaves are tied into formulistic knots and loops, and worn on the head, neck, shoulders, waist, biceps, wrists, and ankles, especially when the magician is actually performing his rite. They give an impressive appearance and inspire confidence.

Another technique of magic involves the use of certain bodily gestures, such as tapping one's body, either in one spot or in many, with a magical object. This is done while the incantation is being recited. There are other body gestures, too, which are not as widely standardized. For instance, there is the tapping of a canoe with a coconut, the rubbing of the belly with a love charm, and the clapping of the hands.

Less important techniques are concerned with direction, space, weapons, food gathering, fire, and symbols of transportation. These are found only sporadically, as in jabbing at the wind or waves with a spear in battling meteorological phenomena, or fishing ritualistically to promote fish for the people of the atoll. In one minor ritual some leaves are burned.

The conventional categories of magic, such as contagious and imitative, have little importance here, for the overwhelming emphasis is verbal. Contagious magic does make an appearance, as when in sorcery a man's rope or clothing is put under a spell, but the use of exuviae, nail parings, hair, or other parts of the intended victim are either uncommon or rare. Imitative magic is more common, as when a magician pretends to step with impunity on sea urchins and fish spines, these being symbolic of the barbs of the black magician; yet it is subordinated to the technique of language.

The Practitioners

Magicians are always part-time specialists and usually men. Women are permitted to be general practitioners in white magic but are denied admittance to the specialized fields, except doctoring. For various reasons, magicians are not often young, this being due in part to the cumbersome character of the taboos imposed on specialists and in part to the jealous guarding of esoteric knowledge by the older men.

In many instances an ordinary person knows magic for his personal use rather than as a profession, and for that reason is scarcely a magician in the strict sense. He is not hired by anyone. He chants to the wind to make it pick up to drive his canoe, and to fish to make them bite. He performs a ritual to cause a girl to love him, and another to make a baby stop vomiting. Magic of this low level is learned from any friend or relative, and in gratitude one rewards him with the usual gifts. The amateur performer of the magic is under no taboos, his person is not sacred, he is unspecialized.

When, on the other hand, white magic is being performed for the benefit of a client, he and the magician are both under constraint to follow certain taboos. In some instances, especially where any of the major categories of magic are being worked, the magician observes additional ones, but ordinarily the following are the general proscriptions that the two must observe: They may not eat certain foods, such as bananas, two kinds of arums, breadfruit, certain small coconuts, chickens, octopuses, land crabs, and certain kinds of fish. They may not enter the sacred garden. Emphasizing the gravity of the situation are still further proscriptions. Neither the specialist nor his client may have sexual intercourse, though ordinarily the latter keeps the taboo even longer than the magician, unless the latter is one of the major kinds of specialists. They may not wash a corpse, dig a grave, or, in certain instances, act as pallbearers. A female client, according to the rules of some magicians, may not visit a menstrual house or be experiencing her menstrual period when the magic is being performed for her benefit. Sometimes a magician demands that his client refrain from coming in contact with salt water or riding a canoe for the duration of the rite. The nature of the taboos and the time they endure are a matter to be decided wholly by the individual magician, but in practice a customary pattern is observed.

One wonders what impels a man to undertake to become a magician when the life he must lead is often extendedly ascetic. In a cultural environment marked by an easy attitude towards life it is incongruous to find men willing to renounce the conventional life for one that is almost monastic. Personal motivations may vary but there is no doubt that two things are operative. The first is a sincere desire to be of service to one's relatives and neighbors. The second is more self-centered and revolves around the great opportunity offered by magic to acquire a "profession" and so bring some distinction to the practitioner. The magician is a man of prestige, and he knows it. His talents enable him to rise above the usual run of people, especially when he does not have inherited political status. He gains considerable satisfaction in the knowledge that he is a person to whom others must go for help. The material compensations are there, too, but they are not the mainspring behind the decision to learn the magical art.

If it can be said that religion is largely dependent on "whom" you know, then it can be said that magic relies on "what" you know, for it is knowledge of the suitable thing to do that brings about the results intended. And so the prospective practitioner must undergo training at the hands of a person versed in the art he wants to acquire.

The relationship between master and pupil is a highly personal one and the ties continue even after the death of the teacher. Magic is a form of property known only to those who have been given a right to share it by virtue of training, friendship, and the payment of gifts. The teacher is either a friend or relative of the pupil. He carefully rehearses his procedures with him. During the period of training, many taboos have to be observed, especially if the magic is of major importance. When finally the student goes out to practice on his own, he may preface his incantation with an appeal to the ghosts of all the men now dead who once knew and used the formula. Here is how one navigator opened his incantation for protection against sorcery:

> You, Weg!
> Look this way from yonder;
> Inform Pul.
> Pul, inform Wasioi!
> May all of you make your wisdom
> effective for me.

The man's teacher was Weg, whose teacher was Pul, whose teacher in turn was Wasioi.

An abbreviated example of the steps undergone in the training of the palm-leaf-knot diviner, a man of uppermost stature, will serve as an illustration of the training of all major magicians. The divination involves the interpretation of combinations of knots tied at random in coconut leaflets. There are 256 possible combinations, each with a meaning for the question posed by the client. The student must learn all the combinations, which are made more complex by the fact that the social status of the client requires varying interpretations, as may also the kind of information asked. The lessons last from one to three months, depending on the aptitude of the learner and other circumstances. Superior intellectual endowments are needed not only to memorize the codes but also to accommodate the answers to given situations. The knot diviners whom I have known—in fact, all the major kinds of magicians I have worked with—displayed impressive mental endowments. The pupil must always compensate his teacher with a gift and continue to show him deference, not only during his lifetime but afterwards as well.

During an apprentice's training to be a diviner he must observe numerous taboos that will remain with him forever. These pertain to menstruation, eating, making fire with wood from a certain species of tree, and approaching a woman drying pandanus leaves over a fire. Certain other taboos last a shorter time. For ten months after the inception of training the pupil may not have sexual relations. For five months, in addition to the permanent taboos mentioned above, there are certain taboos relative to the persons with whom he may eat. The observance of taboos during training is so vital that when a diviner makes errors in his judgments one of the chief causes to which this is attributed is that he failed to observe the taboos. (The failure of any magic, in fact, is often said to be due to the pupil's errancy, although, of course, there are other possible explanations, too.) Not only may the diviner's information to his client be false, but the practitioner may develop depigmentation of the skin and ringworm. The most serious breach of taboo is to indulge in sexual relations. All the taboos pertaining to the diviner are more strictly observed on the island of Mogmog than any other, for this is the center of prestige and authority. The diviners there outrank all others.

Like other major specialists, the knot diviner's status implies a certain degree of sanctity, and no better illustration of this is the inviolability of his person. No one may touch his head, face, and back. If he is seated, it is forbidden for anyone to walk near him in an erect position. Mostly, he eats in solitude, for he may sit down to a meal only with other magicians of primary rank. The fact that a woman has reached the menopause does not exempt her from the taboos of contact. One is reminded of the psychological phenomenon of *noli me tangere,* "do not touch me," sometimes manifested by neurotics. However, the taboos on the person of the magician are designed to protect his power from being endangered by contact with persons of lesser sanctity—a power that is not immanent or charismatic but stems from the possession of knowledge—the knowledge of a ritual. This, in the final analysis, is the source of any magician's power, for to know what to do is the key which unlocks supernatural forces for men.

Areas of Concern

The things that inspire recourse to magic are those about which Ulithians are most anxious.

One of these is the sea. The ocean is a highway for travel and a major source of food, yet at the same time it is inconstant and menacing. So there have to be procedures for minimizing its deleterious phases. Some of the dangers of the deep stem from typhoons; therefore, typhoon magicians exist. Some result from heavy wave action against the shore; for this there are wave specialists to soothe the surface. A constant hazard is present when a vessel tries to achieve a landfall, for not only do storms threaten destruction but the tracklessness of the vast sea presents enormous difficulties in maintaining a proper course; consequently, navigators must fortify themselves not only with help from the god Ialulwe and the ancestral dead but with rituals, talismans, and amulets as well. And then the sea often withholds its fauna from men who search it for fish; to counteract this there are spells, especially in the public interest, for insuring the release of marine creatures.

It is noteworthy that of the four types of primary magicians recognized by Ulithians as being the most elevated of all, each has some involvement with the sea. The typhoon magician is concerned with the effects of giant winds on canoes at sea and in churning up the waters surrounding the islands so that they are threatened with erosion and engulfment. The navigator, half of whose training is in magic, is even more closely oriented towards the sea. The third type of specialist, the community fish magician, has an equally obvious involvement. And the fourth major type, the palm-leaf-knot diviner—engaged in discovering hidden events in the past, present, and future—devotes himself in large part to answering inquiries about the advisability of a voyage, the welfare of sea travelers, and the prospect of catching fish. He encourages decision.

It is firmly believed that much if not most of the threat of the sea originates with men of ill will, residing either within the atoll or without, especially on Yap. Against their nefarious spells, countersorcery must be hurled and objects worn or carried to fend off evil of this nature. The navigator is one of the chief targets of black magic; consequently, he fortifies himself in diverse ways. Here is how a man, who by the way was also a custodian of a shrine for Marespa, endowed a leaf belt with power to protect him:

> I am making an amulet
> Underneath the sky,
> I, the man Chuoior,
> So that I will not die.
> Wave away and empty out (the bad),
> Wave away and put in (the good),
> So that I will not die.
> Where I am standing?
> I stand radiant, glistening radiantly.
> I am a babe in arms,
> The child of Iolofath.
> My food is the incantation,
> My food is the spider lily,
> My food is the coconut offering,
> Of men (who incant against me)
> Anywhere in the islands of Ulithi;
> I will outlive them all.
> Wave away and empty out (the bad),
> Wave away and put in (the good),
> And fence in the shark,
> Make him secure,
> Sew up the tip of his mouth,
> Sew up his bite,
> Sew them up twice.
> The sky is my safeguard,
> The sky is my shield,
> I step on the reef
> And it is shattered.

This was only one of his precautions. Navigators have recourse to many.

Illness is of course a source of much anxious concern, and the native medical practitioner or doctor is understandably ranked high among the specialists in the magical arts. Like the navigator, he employs empirical skills in addition to his supernatural ones, and this may account for the slightly lower ranking that both of them have as compared with the typhoon specialist and the diviner of knots. Besides, much illness is handled by procedures that are neither medical nor pseudomedical. Thus, the diviner has much to say concerning the etiology of a disease and, in addition, he is important to therapy because he often will designate a suitable doctor—a primitive system of referral. Ancestors, as well as a general kind of secondary magician, also to some extent rival the work of the doctor.

The magical aspect of Ulithian medicine stems from the fact that many diseases are believed to be due to sorcery, taboo violation, or other supernatural causes. Most older people have some knowledge of curative spells and so may treat members of the family or friends on an amateur basis. But for graver cases the doctor is summoned. Although he himself is competent to make a diagnosis, he realizes the great importance of etiology in knowing how a disease should be treated; consequently, he may require the help of a knot diviner or a medium to discover the source of the illness.

Anxieties about food account for the plethora of taboos surrounding the swamp garden and the elaborate ritual of the communal fish magician. Of the proscriptions attendant upon the garden, nothing further need be said, but of the fish magician there is much that can be told.

Communal fish magic is carried out once a year by any one of several available men commissioned on behalf of the atoll by the king or the next highest chief on the island of Mogmog. The ritual is always begun on Mogmog, when the moon is full, during either one of two native lunar months corresponding closely to November and December. After preliminaries in which the magician takes a loincloth to the shrine of the ghost of Marespa and another loincloth to the house of the Fasilus lineage, he works magic over the canoe he is going to press into service and then sails across the northern end of the lagoon with four or five assistants until he comes to the island of Song. There he fulfills a duty inspired by a myth explaining the way in which a certain spirit, grateful to a woman for finally yielding to him her yellow wrap-around skirt, reveals the secret of fishing to her in a vision. The spirit is unusual in that he is kind and mellow, whereas sea spirits as a class are greatly feared. His father, however, runs true to form and, being a chief, takes great umbrage at this betrayal. He threatens to harm the woman, so she hides on Song with her husband and two boys. Following the instructions of the kindly spirit, she trains her children in the magic of fishing. Henceforth, all communal fishing magicians must go to Song at the beginning of their extended rite in order to leave her and the sea spirit an offering of two coconuts to help insure the success of the rite, which from this point on departs from the tale and proceeds independently, except to the extent that the magic produced is a fulfillment of the procedures learned from the spirit.

The work of the magician and his assistants is unusually arduous and lasts for two lunar months. They first drag through the water at night a small bundle suspended from the back of the canoe, and attract flying fish to them by light from huge coconut leaf torches. The ingredients of the bundle constitute a strange melange: fruits, roots, bark, the spathes of the coconut and pandanus trees, flowers from the breadfruit tree, soil from a swamp garden, the heads of an eel and scorpion, and termites. Another bundle, filled only with black ants, remains in the canoe. For four days the crew fishes for albacore and tuna in the turbulent waters of Rowaryu channel, facing all weather conditions short of a tropical storm. For the remainder of the two months the fishing continues, but instead of remaining away from Mogmog on the island of Pigelelel, the men return daily to their base in Mogmog. They are surrounded with numerous taboos, the observance of which is eloquent testimony to the unselfish dedication of these men to the common good. The minimal restrictions that all must observe for two months prevent them from walking near any female whatsoever, or having intercourse; going near the menstrual house or talking to its occupants; touching a corpse or digging a grave; eating preserved breadfruit, the fruit of a species of Allophyllus, or the husk of a certain variety of coconut palm; allowing persons who have been in contact with a corpse or have dug a grave during the past five months to handle their food; giving their leftover food to anyone to eat; and sleeping at home. For five months subsequent to the ritual, the men must remain sexually continent. They must continue to live for several days or even months in the men's house, the period of time being optional and a conscious self-abnegation for the benefit of a more successful denouement of the magic. As for the magician himself, his taboos are all of these and many more, and must be observed for four to seven months after the first fishing at the channel. He is virtually a prisoner of his profession. Small wonder that most fish magicians serve a term of only two or three years and then willingly turn over their duties to the next designee.

The gravity of the fishing rite and what it symbolizes may further be seen in the attitude of the community, for during the performance several taboos must be observed by those who merely wait: no one may shout in the men's house, no one may troll for fish in the lagoon, no one may go to Rowaryu channel, and, for the first five days, no relatives of the magician may cut down a live tree.

All these exertions and restraints, briefly alluded to here, speak eloquently of the apprehensions of the people of the atoll towards fish as a source of food, but still more is done than this. Individuals setting out to fish on their own may call for the services of a minor-type fish magician, who performs a simple rite on the canoe to be used and exhorts the fish to come forth to be caught. The performer gets a portion of the catch.

To allay the doubts and frustrations of the lovesick there is a modest body of magic. There are no love magicians as such; instead there are general practitioners in magic who will take on a client with a problem. Most commonly, to insure success in amatory affairs recourse is had to charms. These are usually worn, although sometimes they are kept in one's carrying basket or left in one's house. Men have charms to persuade women, women have similar objects to persuade men. Love charms may take the form of chest bands, head wreaths, neckpieces, and earpieces; the materials used being vines, flowers, leaves, twigs, and roots. Accompanying each charm is an incantation, usually pleading for the charm to cause the loved one to reciprocate one's affection. One might speculate that the relative paucity of magical means for inducing love may be due to the relative ease with which sexual favors are exchanged in the permissive erotic climate of the atoll.

Remaining anxieties are revealed through other minor magicians. Reference has already been made to the wave magician, who soothes the waters if they are too rough for a canoe or if they endanger an island. Measured by his training and the taboos surrounding him he has more stature than other secondary magicians.

Then there is the specialist in spirits such as reside in the larger trees.

His clients are men who are about to cut down a tree and want to have the spirit coaxed into leaving. But it is not clear what anxiety in the realm of reality is relieved by this action, except a generalized fear that disease is often due to the action of tree spirits, who are stubbornly malevolent towards the human race. In 1731 Father Cantova confounded the Ulithians by chopping down a tree whose spirit had killed ten successive people wanting to fell it.

Ulithians are enormously reliant on palm toddy, made from coconut trees. A certain beetle can spoil the sap as it is being allowed to drip into a container fastened to the inflorescence. Therefore, to prevent the awful prospect that one's trees may yield toddy that is ruined, a specialist is impressed into service. Sometimes, if the situation is grave and a whole islet is beginning to feel the effects of the insects, the king may commission the magician to exert his power on behalf of the community.

Canoes constitute valuable property which, because of their fragility and the dangers to which they are exposed, are given the protection of magic exerted by the canoe carpenter, who doubles up in his craftmanship with a knowledge of the suitable rite. The rite is lengthy, which is as it should be, for lineages prize their canoes beyond mere pride of ownership. Although the material accoutrements and body gestures are magical, the rite contains some ingredients of prayer because Solang, who it will be recalled is the patron god of canoe carpentry, is implored to make the vessel lucky, spare it from damage, and cause no one to so admire it as to want to use or even acquire it. Should the canoe, despite the palliatives employed, encounter misfortune, it is believed that Solang is either angry with the canoe carpenter for having violated taboos during the construction of the boat, or with the owners for having failed to give the carpenter proper compensation for his work. Obviously, this way of looking at things serves to promote a satisfactory fulfillment of contractual obligations.

To give peace of mind to owners of a newly built house, a house magician is engaged to bring it good fortune. Some gifts are presented to Thuchera, the god of house carpentry, but as with all gifts offered to spirits, there is always a human who gathers them ultimately into his fold.

Because of a diffuse fear of spirits who moan at night either in the village or the woods, a man who is knowledgeable in these matters protects himself and his family with a spell, which includes throwing a stone in the supposed direction of the spirit.

> *Litingingi! Litingingi!*
> *Letanganga! Letanganga!*
> *Litingingi! Litingingi!*
> *Letanganga! Letanganga!*
> If thou, O spirit, come here
> Near my house
> You will cry out
> *Litingingi! Letanganga!*

There is no use asking what *Litingingi* and *Letanganga* mean. The user of the spell does not know. Chalk it up to the coefficient of weirdness.

Next, there is the grave magician trained to free a burial plot from the spirit residing there so that a corpse may be interred. This again is a response to a generalized fear of spirits as the cause of illness and death. The magician chants,

Scatter from the ground!
Scatter from the ground!
Spirits everywhere,
Whoever you are.
O spirits, halt
Outside my house;
Barracudas of the night,
Sharks of the night,
Halt and soar,
Soar westwards to Palau.

He says this as he circles the ground and jabs it with a dried coconut leaf to whose rib have been tied *ubwoth* leaflets. Part two of the rite involves more pounding with a rock to which more *ubwoth* has been tied. The accompanying words are specifically directed towards the spirits at the grave site.

O Limkhei!
I arrange the ground of
This grave of mine;
Now sleep, sleep, O grave spirits,
Sleep, sleep, O island!
Sleep, sleep, sleep.

Limkhei is variously called the sister of Iolofath or his mother. It is again interesting that a god is drawn into the ritual, but the proposed result is achieved by the performance of the magic, not the salute to the spirit.

Finally, covering all contingencies not specifically embraced by the primary and secondary magicians is a general practitioner, already alluded to, who will work for clients beset by sundry perturbations. Sometimes his work overlaps with that of others who are more specialized. In any event it cannot be said that in Ulithi any area of human anxiety is left unguarded.

Antisocial Rites

Black magic or sorcery is the recourse of men who wish to castigate others whom they feel are guilty of ill will or overt action against them. Such men may not have the power to inflict punishment directly, or may simply wish to conceal their actions from the intended victim and the community. Not much is revealed about the black art because by definition it is criminal in character, and no practitioner is willing to admit his guilt by revealing his knowledge and practice of the forbidden techniques. Still, we are by no means left completely in the dark about the details of sorcery, especially when "reformed" sorcerers are willing to discuss them as if they were hypothetical cases. Insofar as one can focus on so shadowy and outlawed an art, it is utterly conventional.

When a prospective client wishes to engage the services of a professional he must set about cautiously, dropping hints here and there to persons he believes are sorcerers or who may have knowledge of the identity of one. The first man he approaches may pretend not to be a practitioner when in fact he is, so the conversation proceeds cautiously, with much sparring about. If finally the client decides he is indeed talking to a man who practices the art, he delineates his complaint. The sorcerer may decide the aggression is either unwarranted or too severe and will dissuade the person, who will then give him a gift payment in exchange for his silence. The rejected individual may then go off to find someone else to accept his commission. This is not easy, for the sorcerer not only fears the ostracism that would follow exposure but the anger of his intended victim and relatives as well. Besides, there is the danger that the great sky deity, Ialulep, may frown upon his work and inflict harm on him. Once the sorcerer consents to perform, he must be paid in advance with the traditional gifts given to specialists. He then sets out to do what he has been hired to do— cause disease, miscarriages, accidents, death, or other deplorable misfortunes.

The ritual and paraphernalia used, because of their secrecy, are not well known. Yet it seems apparent that the rigmarole is not basically different from that of the white magician. Strangely enough, the sorcerer not only addresses prayers to his teacher's ghost and those of close departed relatives, but to the great god Ialulep as well. The items he uses in his technique may include magical starfish, live lizards, and coconut oil, over which incantations are uttered before the object is buried near the house of the intended victim or, better still, in the floor of the house. Some contagious magic is used, as when the specialist puts a concoction on the person's comb to cause him to contract ringworm, or places it on the garment of the man so that when he puts it on and goes swimming he will be bitten by a shark.

Father Cantova casually mentions while on Ulithi that "there are a few sorcerers, who give us something to do," although he seems to have discredited them. One of them tried to drown the priest and his party by creating a storm as they were returning from an islet where they had taken a census. The typhoon did not materialize. The sorcerer probably did not regard himself as really a sorcerer but as a defender of the pagan faith.

Political sorcery from Gagil district in Yap menaces the atoll when the chiefs there get it into their heads that the people of Ulithi are not being sufficiently obsequious. From the point of view of the Yapese their magic is not truly black, for it is envisioned as a kind of negative sanction against wrongdoers outside their society; from the point of view of their apprehensive vassals, however, nothing could be more darkly tinted.

If this nefarious practice can be epitomized, it can be done through an understanding of certain magical locales, whose generic name need not concern us here. There are three such spots, one on each of the islands of Falalop, Asor, and Sorlen. Ulithians are hazy on the details but say that long ago some men came to the atoll from Gagil and selected these places for their performance of magic. They were empowered by their chiefs on Yap to wreak vindictive magic there whenever they were told to do so. The effects of their sorcery are greatly feared by Ulithians, who attribute to them visitations of respiratory diseases, infestations of crops by insects, and other calamities, including typhoons. The magicians of Yap are considered to be very powerful and are held in considerable awe. In all fairness to the Yapese, however, it should be pointed out that whereas for our present purposes we have stressed the evil side of their magic, they use the same spots and the same magicians to reward Ulithians for being good. This is expressed, for instance, in producing for them an abundance of plant foods or a plethora of fish. However, the lingering impression is not one of gratitude for services of this sort, but dread of the other ones.

Happily, against all the machinations of evildoers in the atoll or without, there are measures to thwart one's enemies. One need not remain a passive victim. There exists a kind of countersorcery that anyone may employ, although in practice it is utilized mostly by the navigator and the communal fish magician. However, the most common device is the amulet, developed to an elaborate degree in the atoll.

When one knows or suspects that sorcery is being directed against him he uses one kind of amulet, and when he merely feels it contingent he uses an amulet belonging to a different native category of such things. The amulet against known sorcery is designed as a specific defense; that against contingent sorcery is a general defense.

Of course sorcery being the clandestine thing that it is, in most instances one can merely defend against the possible rather than the known, so the contingent amulet is the more common. Here there is great variety in the materials used: spider lilies; turmeric; coral, of which there are various colors and shapes; sea urchins; stingers of the stinger ray; leaves of an arum, and so on. The materials are painted in various ways, as with crosses or bands, and are put in various places, depending on the status of the person defending himself. Let us take some examples. A patient is being treated by a magician for an illness resulting from eating tabooed fish while on Yap. The amulet is placed along either of his sides, not to protect him, but to counteract any sorcery being possibly employed against the magician as he works. A canoe carpenter places an amulet under each of the two coconut tree trunks used to support a canoe while it is being built, to ward off any possible threat directed against the execution of his work. One can well imagine how jittery a navigator is about a journey to a distant place, so it should occasion no surprise to know that every navigator worth his salt has at least an amulet tied to the weather platform of his canoe. He cannot afford to take chances against magic. Communal fish magicians are inveterate users of amulets, and, as one might suppose, they place one or more of them in some part of the canoe, such as under the lee platform or the struts on which the sail of the canoe is rested. Ulithians are prone to say that the sorcery they are guarding against emanates on Yap, and to a large extent this is true, but of course it is not considered discreet to imply that Ulithians themselves may be the offenders.

Amulets against sorcery that is known or strongly suspected to be in action against a person are made of the usual materials and are decorated in much the same manner as general amulets.

But the really vital thing about amulets are the incantations that go with them. Amulets for one specific defense and those for another may bear a good deal of resemblance to one another. Anyway, they are not concealed and are often worn on the body, so they can be duplicated or imitated. But the verbal part of the amulet is the secret and powerful part, and employs all the characteristic features of Ulithian magic: the appeal to teacher ghosts, weird words, alliteration and other effects, defiance, boldness, symbolization, and so on. Every incantation is accompanied by appropriate actions.

Social Effects of Magic

If one thinks of magic as a special instrument that supplements the experiential techniques by which life is made possible for Ulithians, it becomes clear that it operates only as an adjunct rather than a primary means. Even then it does not permeate all of life, for it is invoked only as a complement to practical procedures or as a last resort when these utterly fail. If a man makes a journey across the great lagoon, it is enough for him to have a sound canoe and such ordinary nautical skills as paddling, hoisting and lowering a sail, tacking, bailing, and steering. He must know something about currents and the location of protuberances in the reef. Whatever help he uses comes only from someone who assists him in managing the canoe. Even though his destination lies beyond the horizon, he always has some landmarks within his line of vision. Why in the world should he use supernatural aids? He does not. When that same man journeys to Yap or beyond, he must navigate with the stars, worry about set and drift, cope with dead calm or contrary winds, face possible typhoons, and all the other hazards attendant upon a voyage in which there are no guiding landmarks, no chance of paddling or swimming to safety, no help from shore, and possibly not enough food and water to sustain life beyond a week or two. The mariner lacks a compass and a chronometer. All he has besides his craft and skill, as well as the possibility of help from the spirits, is a body of magic and countermagic. He memorizes his spells with meticulous care. He observes all taboos. He takes action beyond the mere exercise of the maritime art.

If one combs further through the areas in which magic is employed, he will find the same consistent strain throughout it all. Take love, for instance. Here there seems to be a reign of unreason. A man may desire a woman who rejects his attentions in favor of an emaciated youth with no particular talent or redeeming personality. He himself is strong, handsome, industrious, loyal, and particularly successful as a fisherman. He has all that a girl would want, or so he thinks. In frustration, since coaxing and appealing to reason have not changed her mind in the least, he takes to consulting an expert in these things and ends up wearing what he hopes will be an amulet to overcome her unreasoned resistance. Instead of suffering the despondency of the unrequited, he now feels he has at least a fighting chance. For reasons that cannot always be fathomed, his suit may eventually turn out to be successful. So he becomes convinced in the efficacy of magic and recommends his specialist to a friend.

Other areas of magic yield similarly to inquiry. A woman wants to gather shellfish and crustaceans stranded on the reef at low tide. No hazards or anxieties beset her and her companions as she walks out and picks them up. They are always there and present no difficulties. To my knowledge, there is no such thing as magic to promote the successful gathering of shellfish and crustaceans on the reef. But for obvious reasons there is elaborate magic to aid in pelagic fishing. The same applies to horticulture. There are some things that grow easily and yield abundantly, so they are raised in routine fashion, but there are others that though prized are unreliable, so they are surrounded with taboos and prescribed rituals. A few effective procedures have been developed to treat illness, but most disease, understandably, resists the impoverished art of the native doctor. Therefore he has to depend a good deal on a superstructure of belief in which, among other things, the etiology, prevention, and therapy of illness lies in the sphere of the magical.

For the Ulithian, when his ordinary cultural techniques and knowledge cannot give him satisfaction, magic rescues him from despair. It seems to bring about results often enough to insure that the principle of extinction through nonreward is not realized. Men do reach distant destinations in safety, lovesick swains do find that the object of their affections reciprocates, fishermen do catch fish swarming onto the reef after months of frustration, one's palm toddy does evade spoilage by invading beetles, and patients do recover from their illnesses. Never mind the failures. They were due to faulty ritual, violation of taboos, or powerful enemies. By providing a course of action, as well as an explanation for misfortune, a man or a whole community can face life with less doubt, less confusion. People may be able to take steps to accommodate themselves advantageously to events revealed by divination. True, there is a price to pay for all this. Many of the anxieties have no basis in reality; instead, they are the very products of the belief in supernaturalism. Furthermore, magic diverts men from the pursuit of logically and pragmatically sound means of overcoming their problems. But until something better comes along, it is good to know that one can tap a power over and above the natural means at one's command. A crew far from home and buffeted by a turbulent sea does not want to be told that its amulets are ineffectual; it cannot wait for the development of secure devices forthcoming in the uncertain future. People must make do with what they have, and if what a Ulithian has are only his palm-leaf knots, his piece of painted coral, and his sting ray effigy to fill out where all his nautical skills and lore have failed him, he is going to turn to them with a confidence that logic cannot demolish.

The magical solution is not the easy one. Magic is a hard master requiring training, the expenditure of human resources, and self-abnegation. It may plunge a whole society into a period of enforced restraint in the firm belief that ritual gains strength when people are willing to deny themselves of their comforts and desires. To be sure, the logic behind a taboo may be lost, as when certain fish are proscribed and certain areas restricted for reasons no one can any longer justify, yet the effect of the whole system of negative rules is to provide such an atmosphere of determination that one can feel every effort is being made to ensure that a rite will not be endangered. Fortified by conformance with the spirit and letter of the restrictive code, the people have an assurance, either individually as clients or collectively as a society, that no stone is left unturned. This gives them the resolution to carry on life instead of lapsing into the paralysis of fear and despondency. Further than this, the taboos of magic serve to emphasize certain important values or areas of life that are not readily apparent or consciously speculated upon.

7

Sexual Behavior

TWO SEEMINGLY OPPOSITE and yet not uncongenial attitudes pervade sexual behavior among the people of the atoll. One is a position of permissiveness; the other is one of restraint.

Sexual abstinence is not viewed as a virtue to be idealized by young people, consequently they do not experience a feeling of shame or guilt when they engage in intercourse before marriage. Women, especially, do not have to satisfy societal moral demands or fortify their chastity by weaving a tissue of ugliness around the sex act. When later they marry they do not carry into their marital union an attitude of revulsion against sex. No ideal is maintained that there is greater happiness and deeper love if the partners in a marriage, especially the wife, have been hitherto completely continent. Lacking such aversion to sexual activity, it consequently follows that there is nothing to inhibit the derivation of pleasure from it. Ulithians maintain ignorance of the phenomena of frigidity and impotence.

When sexual desire is suppressed it is chiefly in conformance with the conviction that there is magic in abstinence. Sexual abnegation fortifies one's effort to harness supernatural forces. The logic behind this is not specifically worked out but would seem to be based on the widely held human premise that self-denial of any kind is a form of sacrifice, and that sacrifice is a price to be paid in return for the use of supernatural power. If sexual self-denial is particularly valued, it may be because of the recognized power of sex in procreation.

Other than ritualistic restraints there are those having to do with marriage, kinship, and reproduction, as well as political status vis-à-vis Yap. They are aimed not at sex as such but in preventing the disruption of the balance of social relationships through competition for sexual partners.

And so, despite the leniency with which sexual gratification is viewed, sexual license or promiscuity, even among the unmarried, is far from being a socially sanctioned custom of the society.

77

Views on Sex and Decency

The Ulithian does not speculate a good deal on the matter of sex. He has built up almost no explanations or rationalizations regarding the differences between men and women and their impulses and genital organs. He is well aware of the reproductive role of sex but thinks little more about the matter than to notice the connection.

To him, love is an emotional attachment ranging over a wide spectrum, so that it encompasses an attitude towards a sweetheart, a child, a parent, a dog, or even a canoe. The seat of love is vaguely localized in a spot just below the ensiform process of the sternum. When the emotion has sexual connotations it travels down to the genitals. The unerotic feeling of love that one has, however, for other persons or things does not go down to the genital area, because the attraction is different. It is said that the sensation of sexual love which men and women have towards one another is due to a spirit, but the spirit is never identified or described, and no ideas are held as to its sex or place of abode. As far as terminology goes, then, no distinction is made in terms of logic, except that sexual love extends to the primary erogenous zone.

Sex is not clearly idealized. There is not even a consistent concept as to what the ideal sex partner ought to be like. Personal taste rather than a cultural ideal seems to dictate what is desirable. Outright ugliness is of course recognized by everyone, but whether a slender or heavy person, a tall or short one, has more appeal depends on the individual. It is worth mentioning that there is no cultural ideal concerning the pneumatic breasted woman. In fact, Ulithian men wonder why foreigners make such a to-do over breasts; they claim not to find them stimulating.

Definite ideas are maintained regarding decency and decorum. Men always wear a loincloth, but an upper garment is considered improper and is nonexistent. However, to guard against rain a cape as well as a leaf hat may be employed. Men never expose their privates in the company of women and are even reluctant to do so freely among men, being especially careful not to be seen naked by their children.

Women wear a short wrap-around skirt of woven hibiscus and banana fiber extending to the knees, and nothing more. To attempt to wear something covering the breasts is an act of immodesty or a breach of convention; in any event it is not done. Prior to puberty a girl wears a "grass" skirt made of shredded coconut leaflets or pandanus. Undergarments are not part of traditional dress. As for exposure, women are expected to exercise more care than men in keeping themselves covered in the proper places. It is not immodest for women to expose themselves in one another's presence, but it is not commonly done.

Nudity among children is the rule, continuing until about the age of five or six. People are utterly indifferent to nudity in children of such early age, but are insistent on scrupulous observance of modesty in clothing after that.

Decency must be maintained in other ways. It is considered highly improper for certain persons of opposite sex to be seen together. Such persons include especially those who stand in a real brother and sister relationship. They must avoid one another if they are the only ones present in a place, and, in a group, they may not sit around if matters of sex are under discussion, either seriously or jokingly. The rule of avoidance is a severe one, and if a sister stumbles upon a brother in the woods or must pass by him unavoidably, she must signal her presence with a certain phrase and pass by at as discreet a distance as possible. Patterned avoidance behavior is also expected of brothers and sisters whose relationship is only classificatory, except that the avoidance is less stringent. In such tiny islands, where so many people call one another by sibling terms, such relaxation of the rules is clearly imperative. Aside from brothers and sisters, it is considered bad taste for an unrelated man and woman to be alone in places where others may see them. If they want to be together, this is permissible as long as they are discreet about being detected; there is no inquiry into the motives of couples who meet in secret.

In bathing and elimination, complete care must be taken to see that one is not observed by a person of the other sex. Women who bathe in the sea, as they often do several times a day, do so in broad daylight, but always wearing their skirts. Those who bathe on land do so just before daybreak or after sunset and, unless their privacy is completely assured, they keep their skirts on. Women may bathe in concert, experiencing no feeling of shame or immodesty in doing so. Even in eliminating, women feel no shyness in the presence of other women; but they do take precautions not to be seen by men. As for men, all the precautions expected of women are also to be taken by men, except that they are not expected to exercise quite the care as a woman in intruding on a person who is bathing or eliminating. Women, whether they are the intruders or the intruded upon, feel the greater embarrassment. Notwithstanding, even though it is considered improper for a person of one sex to witness a person of the other sex in the act of bathing or eliminating, such an offense is not the traumatic event it would be in some other societies.

Women watch out for their modesty in other ways too. They do not climb trees, because of the possibility that a passing male might glance upward and espy their intimate anatomy. When women sit down, they keep their skirts adjusted and their legs crossed or close together. When men and women are in the confining quarters of a canoe at sea, the matter of preserving modesty becomes a difficult one. In getting on a canoe, a woman must not climb; she must give a short leap upward and land on the edge of the canoe in a seated position. Women become expert at doing this gracefully. When she gets off, she slides off with her legs close together. The matter of elimination is a special problem during a trip. Should a women have to urinate during a short trip, she must do everything she can to restrain herself, but if that is not possible she takes other measures. She sits down in the bottom of the canoe and throws sea water over her body, pretending to be bathing, and while doing this she urinates. Then she bails out the water. On a short trip a woman does not defecate. The rule appears to be immutable, and a woman must take meticulous care to see that when she boards a canoe she has forestalled the possibility of later embarrassment. When women accompany men on long voyages they stay in a cabin over the leeward platform and eliminate through a specially built hole in the platform.

As for a man, when starting out in a small canoe for a short trip, he takes all precautions ahead of time to see that he does not have to eliminate during the voyage if women are to be present. Should he be forced to urinate, he dives into the water on one pretext or another, such as to recover an oar or a bailer. On long trips, since large canoes are equipped with cabins, men have the women stay in the cabins and they then eliminate over the side of the canoe from a squatting position on the edge of the hull.

In mixed company there are numerous restrictions on the use of words connected with sex and elimination. In many instances, euphemisms and circumlocutions may be substituted. Thus, one does not mention the bat, because this is a figure which is tattooed on women's legs; instead, one speaks of the rat. One does not use the word for dark red, because this is the color of the vagina; instead, one uses the general term for red. One does not speak directly of a loincloth, which may be either the garment of a man or a woman; instead, one speaks of banana bark when referring to a man's breechclout, and hibiscus when speaking of the female garment, these being the names of the materials utilized in their manufacture.

Again, in mixed company, certain words involving sex and the organs of sex have no substitutes and must be altogether avoided. They include the words for penis, vagina, clitoris, semen, testes, coition, masturbation, and many others. Terms pertaining to elimination have such substitutes as "going to the beach" or "lightening oneself" for defecation, and "standing water" for urinating. However, there are no substitutes for feces or urine, unless these refer to the excrement of children, in which instance certain special terms are used.

In the presence of elders, towards whom Ulithians always maintain an attitude of enormous respect, many of the terms pertaining to sex and elimination must similarly be avoided, even if the company is not mixed. They include the words for the sex organs and their areas, as well as terms for the rectum, feces, urine, petting, coition, masturbation, and breaking wind.

When a person violates the restrictions on coarse words, he is met with a disapproving silence. A repeated offender is regarded as a foul-mouthed sort of person, improperly brought up. He may be scolded by his elders or a chief.

In conformity with their subordinate status, women are expected to observe a certain etiquette towards members of the opposite sex. They do not intrude in groups where men are working or talking. In walking with men, they follow submissively at the rear. If it is necessary for them to sit with men, they make themselves unobtrusive and do not enter into conversations unless necessary. At any rate, they must always act shy and modest in public, because forward women are bad women. Even in the intimacy of the sexual act, they must remain passive. Much of the bashfulness that women display in public, however, is a cultural pose. What passes for outward shyness may only be assumed coyness. In conversation this often is expressed in the form of a soft, whining tone —almost a falsetto. Another pose that women may assume in public when men are about, is one of great boredom or indifference to their surroundings.

Erotic Expression and Stimulation

In inquiring into the extent to which the people express themselves with regard to sex, one finds a complete absence of direct sexual symbolism in their representative art. It must be borne in mind, however, that there is almost no representative art, anyway. But the small amount that does exist is devoid of phallic symbols and sex themes.

It is a different story with women's tattooing, which while confining itself to geometric designs tends to have strong sexual connotations. This stems from the fact that women tattoo their thighs, groins, and labia minora. The tattooing of the last is done with a solid black pigment and is purportedly done for modesty's sake, to conceal the red membrane of the vaginal orifice during sex play. Regardless of the veracity of this explanation, which seems farfetched but is stoutly insisted upon, the fact remains that women's tattooing is not a subject to be discussed in public. As for men's tattooing, there is no erotic counterpart, for it is never done in the more intimate parts of the anatomy and is completely unconcealed. It has no sexual connotations.

Preoccupation with sex manifests itself clearly in the dance. There are three main categories of dances in which eroticism is apparent. These dances utilize almost twenty standardized movements, each with a name. Some of these movements are clearly erotic. Thus, the slapping of the buttocks, the thrusting of the pelvis back and forth with the legs wide apart in a deep bend, and the twisting of the hips from one side to another, are unmistakeably sexual in intent. Other movements, in which the biceps are slapped, the arms outstretched to simulate a bird in flight, or the head shaken or nodded, have no sexual meaning of themselves but may be executed in an erotic setting. Only one category of the dance, except for a stick dance alleged to have been imported from Yap, is devoid of sex or obscenity, so that it is safe to make the generalization that dancing is commonly concerned with sex. This is corroborated by the fact that the dances in question, with one notable exception, are performed segregated, so that women are enjoined from viewing men and vice versa.

Songs accompany the erotic dances, and these are bolder than the gestures that accompany them. It is likely that the words are more influential than the movements in requiring the separation of the sexes during the performance of the restricted dances.

Ulithians have love songs that do not necessarily accompany the dance, and most of these are essentially poetic and tender, though more straightforward than would be conventional in Western society. Such songs may be sung publicly or in the intimacy of two lovers' company. When sung by a group, the group is either all male or all female. Songs of this nature are sometimes sung by a person as a means of whiling the time away while at work or sailing in a canoe.

An outrageously indecorous dance with lewd words has already been referred to in connection with the quasi-legal conventionalization of diffuse sanctions against persons in need of castigation. It is the *hamath*. This dance is performed on peculiarly disparate occasions, having an interconnection through their relationship to the great god Iongolap. When used as a corrective it employs songs of criticism by men against women, and vice versa. It is a battle of derogatory taunts which may start against a single individual but ultimately widens its scope so as to become part of the war of the sexes. The words are straightforward, bitter, and obscene. Thus, if a woman is being attacked, her name is mentioned without evasion, and she may be accused of having an odd-sized sex organ or a large rectum. The dancers may tell how often they have creeped up to her as she lay asleep, and tickled her vagina. She may be accused of masturbating and performing *fellatio*. As the song is being sung, the reason for the attack on the woman is revealed, be it for laziness, shrewishness, adultery, and so on. When women take their turn with the dance they retaliate in kind. Sexual alignments and sexual ridicule play the main part in the performance.

Ulithian curses and profanity are overwhelmingly lewd. When a person is provoked and wishes to vent his aggression on another, he resorts to obscenity rather than to supernatural damnations or blasphemy. Typical insults are: "Your father's rectum!" "Inside your mother's eye!" "Come eat my behind!" "Go lay with your sister!" "Your mother's pubic tattooing." Such expressions may be hurled in anger by a man or a woman, modifications of course being made to suit the sex of the person under assault. Men use profanity more than do women. It is not uncommon among children, even when they are but a few years of age. Actually, the epithets are so highly stereotyped that their content is not as important as the anger behind them. They do have a certain amount of force, but it would be a mistake to impute excessive aggression to the people of Ulithi on account of them. The notable thing is that instead of expressing a desire for the death, sickness, or damnation or a person they taunt him with obscenities.

Reference may be made to the sexual content of traditional narrative, where love, incest, and lewdness are by no means uncommon. There is no particular concern over the presence of children in the audience; indeed, most often the ones to whom the tales are told are children. Scatology runs rampant in a story centering around a "heroine" called Feces Girl. As the story is told, the word for feces is mentioned incessantly without euphemism. Feces Girl is ugly and when she walks she is followed by flies. For some inexplicable reason, some men come to fetch her to be the bride of the son of a chief. As she leaves her island she must bid farewell to every pile of ordure there, and her adieu is carefully repeated by the narrator for each pile. She overlooks one pile, however, and later on it vengefully causes her to turn completely into excrement. Laughter greets the details of this odiferous narrative. In a story that apparently stems from a true incident, a hero lies unconscious in a refuse pit, where he had been thrown and beaten by some men, and he is revived when during the night a woman comes there and urinates on him. He returns to the atoll of Ifaluk, his home, and there he causes his penis slowly to become erect, and as the people watch, they see that it points in the direction of Woleai. This is his way of informing the people where they are to go to do battle against his assailants. A story about an ogre ends with two young sisters pulling his guts out of his anus as they sing a song taunting him about his breaking wind. Another one has a father discover that his daughter has been eaten by an ogre, after he has felled the monster; as the latter lies there the father sees his daughter protruding from the ogre's anus.

One should not get the impression that the tales are excessively colored with such coarse details. Many of them are yarns delineating amusing amatory episodes. Some deal with incest, at times lightly, as when two brothers trick their sister into sleeping with them, and at times seriously, as when the parents of two exceedingly handsome children decree that they must marry one another because they will be unable to find mates equally as handsome as they. An oedipal story, probably genetically related to the Greek story of Oedipus, has an incest theme, but here, as in other accounts involving sexual relations between those within a proscribed range, matters are always resolved in a pleasing manner.

Many erotic tales told on Ulithi are candidly romantic in nature. One, involving a youth separated from his sweetheart, who dies from pining while he is away on a voyage to Fais, is marked by compassion and tragedy, for he himself dies grieving for his loved one. Another, in which a youth marries a girl who has descended from the Sky World in a swinging bed, is filled with the pangs of frustration and separation because a covetous chief sends the husband away in order to seize the wife for his own lecherous designs. In the end, after some tender episodes in which she endeavors to hint to her despondent husband that she has returned to him, they are tearfully reunited and the evil chief is killed by a friendly spirit. Ulithi has a "swan maiden" type of story, in which a young man marries and then loses a girl who has come ashore as a porpoise to watch a dance and becomes transformed into a woman by removing her tail. Not to prolong these examples unduly, one final story may be mentioned. In it a young man is ordered to marry an old and ugly woman, and he does so without showing any sign of resentment. Indeed, he treats her with every consideration, and one day, in reluctant response to her cryptic urgings, he cuts off her head and she stands there a dazzlingly pretty girl. Another man has been ordered to marry an even older woman but does so with bad grace. When he learns about the transformation of his friend's wife, he cuts off his own wife's head, but not at her demand, and she turns out even older than ever and too feeble to walk, so he must carry her through the village on his back, to the derision of the people.

In these stories, then, sex appears in a wide range. In some of them words are not minced and are even injected for shock effect. For the most part, sex is treated routinely, and certainly without prudery. There is a constant theme of marriage, pregnancy, and birth, followed by another marriage, pregnancy, and birth—as if this were a way of marking the passage of time. The heroes and heroines may be far from perfect, and often, as in the case of Iolofath, are adulterous, but to compensate for this there are lovers whose ideals, emotions, and travails are not at all unlike those of Western romances.

Turning back to reality instead of fantasy, sex is a common subject for jesting and conversation, and when young men are with others of their age they are apt to expand upon their past exploits and their future aspirations in the arena of love. Young girls do the same. The anecdotes that are told are not standardized pieces of fiction to entertain one's friends; despite embellishments, they are true accounts. My chief informant told me an experience he was fond of relating to others. Once, when his wife was confined to a menstrual house away from their isle, and he felt a desire for feminine companionship, he encountered an unfamiliar girl on a path and arranged for a tryst that night. But while waiting for darkness he fell asleep in the clubhouse. A friend of his, also on the prowl for a girl, stumbled upon her at the appointed place and realizing that she was looking for his friend, imitated his voice and succeeded in making love to her without her discovering he was an imposter. Then he returned exultantly to the clubhouse and told the sleepy friend of his success of the evening. My informant denied that he had made arrangements for a rendezvous, but then confessed, whereupon his friend told him that all was not lost as he had arranged a meeting for the next night and my informant could keep the appointment. He did. He made love to the unsuspecting girl. Then he told her the details of the previous night, and she became so angry she would not accept his apology and refused ever to see him again.

This story is repeated here only to give some flavor of the kind of anecdote that amuses Ulithians. Two more may be added in more condensed form. The same men in the previous escapade made love one night to two girls in their house. Exhausted, they fell asleep, but one man awoke in time to leave, while my informant remained asleep. About daybreak he cried out in his sleep and people came running posthaste to see what the trouble might be. They entered the house and saw the bewildered young man. Later, the two friends met and after some preliminary recriminations on the part of the embarrassed youth, he and his friend fell into convulsions of laughter. Another anecdote, involving a different young man, tells how he overslept in his girl friend's house after making love to her during the night. The other people in the house saw them at daybreak but left quietly so as not to embarrass them. But the boy had to remain indoors the rest of the day, hiding up in the rafters, so no visitors would see him, and was not able to leave until nightfall. Such are the precious experiences that Ulithians like to swap with one another, and they do so with the feeling that sex can be droll.

Psychosexual stimuli are of course initiated, in varying degrees, by dances, songs, storytelling, and jesting. These activities may serve successfully as stimulants for sexual congress, and at the same time in some instances present the opportunity for furthering amourettes. Thus, a dance may start out as a village affair, but when it is over the younger people will linger on into the night and often wander into the woods in pairs.

There is an institutionalized occasion for sexual stimulus, however, that goes beyond anything so far discussed. It is the holiday known as *pi supuhui,* or a hundred pettings.

This holiday involves all persons of the village who are not excessively old or young. It occurs at no set intervals, and is unconnected with a feast or other event; rather, it takes place at the suggestion of a group or individual.

What happens is that couples of opposite sex, regardless of age, pair off and go into the woods for picnicking, relaxation, and merriment. If it is night, as it more commonly may be, the pairs prefer canoe sheds. Married couples are not allowed to go off together. One's partner, who may be unmarried or married, is never a relative. However, one does not remain with the same partner throughout the occasion, and "tagging" is practiced so that it will not seem, however true it may be, that two persons are particularly attached to one another. If visitors from other communities happen to be present at the time, they are invited to join in. Men invite female visitors to be partners, and females invite males. Should there be a discrepancy in the sex ratio, a man or woman is shared. Small children pair off, too, but they are usually made to keep at a discreet distance from their elders. The play of these children is noncoital and considered to be innocuous, as it usually is, but it may go so far as to imitate the amorous words, caressing, and embracing of men and women. Youngsters may even explore one another's genitals. Group dances sometimes take place, but they are spontaneous and not instigated by someone in authority. Either before or after the main part of the holiday there is a group feast, fish having been caught beforehand by the men and cooked by the women. The *pi supuhui* is one of the rare occasions when erotic dances are performed in mixed company. No conflict results from this institutionalized departure from conventional behavior, and while certain liberties may be taken, the prevailing spirit is one of affection rather than license. The people describe it as "nice play" and make no apologies for it.

Heterosexual petting is of course most commonly pursued outside this sporadic institutionalized setting. It involves many kinds of physical contacts producing sexual arousal. The male undertakes the preponderance of the action, which usually begins with hugging and close body contacts of a general nature. There is no lip or tongue kissing; instead, there is a rubbing of noses, which may be construed as a mild equivalent. Nor is there oral or manual manipulation of the female breasts. Ulithians maintain that neither the mouth nor the breasts are erogenous, and have backed up their conviction, misguided as it may be, with failure to develop erotic techniques employing them. Moral reasons are not involved, and it is noteworthy that the same people who raise queries about the lips and breasts have no objection to genital appositon. There is, however, moral objection to oral-genital activities, which are considered lewd. The one positive function of premarital petting is that it provides young people with an opportunity to learn something about sexual arousal and the art of love. In a society which does not consider erotic feelings sinful, it is educational because it permits them to adjust both sexually and socially to a person of the other sex without the inhibiting force of social condemnation. Early petting provides young people with a chance to sample a variety of persons of the other sex and to arrive at some kind of preference that will ultimately be of use in selecting a marriage partner. Marital petting of course serves different functions and is most often employed as enjoyable coital play, but it does not substitute for coitus as a source of orgastic satisfaction.

Sexual stimulation of a mild sort comes from another source, namely, the use of ornaments, clothing, and fragrant odors. A person makes himself appealing by wearing a wreath or covering himself with turmeric. Pleasant smelling flowers, leaves, fruits, and plants are worn to attract members of the opposite sex. Women are allowed almost no latitude in the color and design of their skirts but they may tighten them or loosen them for desired effects on men. Tattooing of the groin or labia minora is considered to be not only something to promote modesty, but, as claimed, a sexual stimulant for men, and women are said to be very well aware of this.

The use of love charms has already been alluded to. Women sometimes perform love magic over food which a man is about to eat. Men may whisper an incantation over tobacco being presented to a loved one as a cigarette. There is no concept of aphrodisiacs.

Certain acts may be interpreted, in the proper context, as sexual overtures. There is nothing startling about them, but they are fairly common techniques. Suggestive gestures consist of rolling of the eyes, a quick raising of the eyebrows, a wink, an outward flick of the tip of the tongue, a sly click of the tongue, a faint toss of the head, a stare, a scratch of the head, a scratch of the palm or pinch of the hand when exchanging an article, and so on.

Coition and Its Rules

Coition is regarded as a highly pleasurable activity and is not beclouded with feelings of guilt or disgust. It is considered as something necessary, not only to satisfy a natural desire for physical and emotional gratification, but also to have children. Some believe it leads to colds, laziness, weakness, retardation of growth, discoloration of the skin, and other undesirable conditions, but this attitude is by no means a prevalent one and prevails usually when extraneous factors creep in. Under certain conditions, of course, sexual congress is regarded as ritually unclean. So, despite its acceptance as a desirable experience, it is felt that certain rules regarding it should be observed.

In the regulation of coition, place and time are matters to be taken into account. Intercourse is carried out either in the house or in the woods, whether or not the couple is married. Unmarried lovers may sleep in one another's houses, though this is done secretly and under cover of darkness. Some parents become angered if lovers are discovered in the house, but others ignore their presence. The really essential precaution, as with everything else in Ulithi, is to be discreet. It is strictly forbidden to have intercouse in the men's council house, and it is unthinkable to perform the act in the menstrual house.

The time of copulation is controlled by certain regulating factors. One type of restriction is the magico-religious taboo. These limitations, which have been amply described in connection with the performance of magic by specialists and their clients, may be severely restrictive. Another set of limitations is operative in connection with the washing and burying of a corpse. The same period of sexual restraint must also be observed by all close relatives who are in mourning. Taboos exist for a woman during a lengthy period following parturition. They are also in effect during the time of her menses, when she is confined to the menstrual house. Certain restrictions of course exist with respect to kinship. As for rules concerning the time of day when copulation may occur, none exist, although practicality makes it more common during nighttime, when greater privacy is assured.

In coitus the man is expected to take the initiative. It is improper for the woman to make advances, and should she do so her actions would be regarded as evidence of excessive pruriency. Preliminary petting is usually resorted to before the act is consummated, especially with young lovers. The play element is stressed, with the boy perhaps teasing the girl by pulling out a pubic hair or the girl assuming a pretense of untoward hostility. A practice found elsewhere in the Carolines is present here and consists of the male prodding the female clitoris with his phallus over a prolonged period of time before making entry. The practice is not, however, developed into the kind of game reported for Truk.

Circumstances may dictate the coital position, but the one that is preferred is a recumbent one with the partners face to face and the man superior. Sometimes an averse position is used, with the woman lying ventrally or with both partners positioned laterally. But common for couples pressed for time or without the comforting reassurance of proper concealment is an averse position in which entry from the rear is effected while the woman is standing bent over or kneeling.

Extravaginal coitus is known but not common, being regarded with ridicule and disapprobation. Penile-vaginal copulation is considered normal and best.

The duration of coitus is short and lasts approximately the length of time it takes the male to reach his climax, no attempt being made to prolong the act. However, coitus may be repeated several times at one session. It may very well be that the unfavorable circumstances prevailing on a small island, where privacy is not easily gained, have militated against extending the act unduly and that this has caused the development of a pattern or rule that might never have come into being if matters were otherwise. Women seem to have no difficulty in achieving the climax. The man makes no special effort to time his movements so as to induce simultaneous orgasmic satisfaction, and there is no particular premium placed on the order in which the climax is reached. The women heightens her partner's satisfaction by contracting her vaginal muscles, an act referred to as "spirit."

There is no recourse to contraceptive measures. No mechanical or medicative devices for preventing conception exist, and coitus interruptus is not practiced. Informants are insistent on this score, and there is no reason to doubt their veracity.

Impotence is rare, and its presence has even been denied. Frigidity among women is not common, and in discussing this matter with some men, one of them doubted the possibility that it could exist in a female population so ardent. However, his sampling may have been biased.

Heterosexual explorations begin early in the preadolescent years among companions of approximately the same age. With nudity the rule for all children in their first years, genital differences as well as differences in urination postures, are observed from the very beginning. Genital exhibition is thus rendered meaningless, and the children proceed directly to the inspection of one another's sexual parts. Manipulation is usually confined at first to mere touching and does not ordinarily develop into truly mastabatory contacts. Where there is manual manipulation the erotic implications of the sex play may go unrecognized. Mouth-genital contacts appear to be rare, but genital apposition is not uncommon. Having in many instances witnessed copulation by their parents, the children may make clumsy efforts at penetration, but vaginal entries are rare and limited for the most part to finger insertion. Much of the sex play of young children comes when they are in mixed groups and have occasions to pair off, as when playing a game of hide-and-seek. There may be some hugging and tickling, and by the time of adolescence this may become a light petting.

When coition itself is eventually engaged in, it is again at an early age. It is not thought of as associated with any necessary commitment to marriage; indeed, it is regarded as a thing apart. Courting follows a pattern, in which tentative advances are followed up with an exchange of gifts and declarations of affection. Ordinarily, one's first partner is an experienced person; novices do not often initiate one another. Adults attempt to restrain children from engaging in sexual activity only to the extent that their actions would violate the rules of incest and decorum. Their surveillance is strictest when enforcing the rule of brother-sister avoidance, which is aided by enforced segregation in sleeping. Otherwise, it is largely confined to building up a general climate of discretion that will enable the young people to avoid inviting the barbs of derogation, which may come from the community if the boy or girl act too boldly or intemperately.

It may be said that premarital liaisons are so common that they constitute the rule. The number of people who enter into a marriage with at least one sex experience behind them is overwhelming. Only because of some unusual circumstance, as in the rare event that a girl has been betrothed while still a child, would one of the partners in a marriage be virginal. Premarital affairs, then, are socially accepted and, in fact, even advocated by many people on the grounds that, if confined to a single lover, they reduce conflict within the community. Promiscuity is frowned upon; it is believed to promote barrenness in a girl and to betray a defect of character. Even if quite attractive, an indiscriminate girl is less desirable as a marital partner than one who shows a certain degree of fidelity toward her lover. The same applies to a promiscuous boy. It is said that not only will he prove unfaithful but may become sterile through his inconstancy.

Formal sanctions are never imposed by the community against premarital liaisons. However, if the boy or girl involved is lazy, irresponsible, and uncooperative, he or she may be the recipient of unfavorable gossip. In some instances the boy is censured by the council of male elders and the girl by the council of women, the action of these bodies being the closest approach to a public expression of disapprobation. The immediate family, too, may express its disapproval if the person is very young or excessively promiscuous, giving him a stern warning or a tongue lashing, or even a beating.

Rivalry is common in premarital sex relations, but good taste dictates that the matter shall not end in blows. At most, there may be a quarrel or a prolonged grudge. Rivals for a girl may talk over the matter and decide that one of them will leave the field clear for the other. Should it be impossible to reach an agreement, the rivals may compete for the girl's favor by giving her gifts and added attention, as well as trying to outdo one another in dress and ornamentation.

Extramarital relations are common, but while ordinarily they are frowned upon by society there are situations in which they are permitted. Two men may promote and cement their friendship by an occasional exchange of spouses, the wives consenting. The attitude of the community toward this practice is a tolerant one.

Instead of such exchange, sexual hospitality may be practiced when visitors come from other islands and are without women, whether because they are separated, divorced, or widowed, or their wives are indisposed. The man lending his wife is a close friend of the recipient, who does not make a payment for the favor but is disposed to present a gift of appreciation to the husband. The whole practice is regarded as a splendid gesture and is not disparaged in principle.

Less nobly motivated than this is the surrendering of a wife to a man in exchange for a gift payment, the two men not necessarily being close friends. The wife is usually especially attractive and the man desiring her more or less homely. The practice never rises to the full status of prostitution, and in any event the wife's permission is always necessary. Her husband does not offer her for payment more than once or twice a year, especially since her family would not tolerate it if it should learn about the transaction. Sometimes the couple is not particularly interested in one another, and so the wife is indifferent about the morality of the situation, as is her husband. While this occasional, part-time kind of prostitution has been reported to me as a possibility, no one seems to have heard of its practice in many years. Certainly, it is not institutionalized.

Adultery is so common as to seem to be within the range of permissibility, but it is not. Virtually all married people are guilty of it. It is said to be committed for the thrill which accompanies variety and the forbidden, but often it is a way of evening a score with an adulterous spouse. Adultery is not looked upon any more lightly in the case of a man than in that of a woman. It constitutes grounds for divorce as much for the one as the other. The community takes no steps to punish it, except indirectly through gossip. The family of the guilty party takes a more direct interest, and the parents or older brother may even resort to a beating. In contrast to this, the injured spouse is surprisingly restrained and may at first do no more than issue a warning to the paramour and a tongue lashing to the spouse. On rare occasions, where there is persistent adultery, blows may follow, but it is hard indeed to document this recourse in a society so deprecatory of violence. To prevent adultery, few steps are ever taken. One spouse may watch over the other with special care, but he or she places few restrictions on the other's movements. Chaperoning is unheard of. It is not in good taste to act as informer against guilty persons. Unless they are very close friends or relatives of the injured party, informers are considered troublemakers.

Matters of adultery are kept within private bounds as much as possible, it being especially indiscreet to speak about them publicly, for despite the frequency of extramarital relations, marital fidelity is the social ideal.

The grand rule above all others limiting sexual gratification is that of incest, a practice viewed with thorough revulsion by Ulithians. All blood relatives, unless they are so distantly related to one another that the relationship is vague, come under this restriction. All lineage mates fall under the taboo, and so do relatives by adoption, even though they are not blood relatives. Included are all classificatory parents, siblings, and children—a wide range of people. But affinal relatives are not included, so that it is not incestuous to have sexual congress with a wife's mother, sister, or daughter by a previous marriage, though such sex relations are forbidden on other grounds. Incest is indeed rare, and when it occurs is usually found on the outermost ranges involving classificatory relatives rather than close ones.

According to native belief, the physical results of incest are illness in either the offenders or their close relatives. This illness is the result of the work of ancestral ghosts and takes the form of headaches, boils, or yaws. It is said that the child of an incestuous marriage will be mentally deficient, its toes webbed together, its fingers twisted and bent, and its buttocks shriveled. The overt social penalties of incest are minimal, with no physical action on the part of society, which is content to satisfy itself with resentment and ridicule. I knew of one incestuous marriage, in which the partners were only distantly related, yet the couple was ostracized. In an unusual display of resentment over the incestuous activity of a married man, the men of the village of Mogmog considered killing the culprit—a rare reaction for a people as restrained as the natives of the atoll. Children born of incestuous unions are treated with the customary sympathy extended to all children born of illegitimate liaisons. Ulithians feel that illegitimate children are guilty of no wrongdoing and should be cared for just as other children, and be allowed to take their place in society without penalty to them.

Looking back over all these attitudes and practices, the question may be raised as to the effects of such permissiveness. In replying to this query it should be kept in mind that despite the leniency with which sexual activities are viewed, there are always controls. These exist even for unmarried adolescents, who must observe not only the regulations pertaining to incest but those of decorum and moderation as well. Extramarital relations are not at all permitted to go uncontrolled. Though wife lending is allowed, it is always with the consent of both the husband and the wife. Sexual relations between a man and his wife's sister is permitted under some occasional circumstances. Postmarital affairs are conducted mostly by older people in the society and therefore are not viewed with disapproval, except to the extent that they involve married partners. For such persons as mourners, lactating mothers, supernatural specialists, and others in a special ritual status, there is an even more excessive burden of continence and avoidance. So on the one hand there is the bait of permissiveness, and on the other the cold facts of regulation.

There is more, too. Rivalries, frustrations, unrequited affection, and lack of privacy put obstacles in the way of simple sexual fulfillment. Take the matter of privacy. It is sometimes difficult to consummate the sexual act in the woods, for there is not a good deal of concealment in the daytime and there is a fear of spirits at night. Houses do not afford a good deal of privacy, visual or aural. Frustration also comes from the separations brought about by the frequent moving about of Ulithians. They go from one island to another for extended periods of time, and often leave the atoll to visit distant places, being gone for months or even years. This discourages an incipient alliance, and usually terminates one that is in full bloom. A further situation conducive to frustration is the customary segregation of the sexes outside the family circle. Women work and amuse themselves in their own groups, and men in theirs. There is not a good deal of commingling in public.

A fact of demography conducive to the absorption of the mind in sexual matters is the inordinate limit on potential sexual partners. In a society where kinship is extended to include a very wide range of persons, and where there is almost no single person beyond teen age, the number of individuals available as sex mates is severely circumscribed. One young man wanted to remarry after a divorce but had only three women in the whole atoll available to him. He rejected two because they were pretty and would probably prove unfaithful, and married the third, an older and unattractive widow with a child. With individuals forced by circumstances such as this to enter into opportunistic or arranged marriages, a man may later feel impelled to find satisfaction with a woman more desirable to him than his wife. She may similarly feel that she can gain greater satisfaction in an extramarital relationship. The sense of excitement going with an illicit relationship is an additional incentive spurring people into adultery.

Thus, amidst an atmosphere of sexual leniency there are rules of restraint, but they do not impose abstinence to the extent that it has deleterious effects on the normal functioning of the organism. Abstinence is not idealized and is practiced only to a moderate degree by most people, particularly the young. This has the effect ultimately of reducing sexual phantasies among them and probably is instrumental in reducing physiological and psychological disturbances as well. In substantiation of this point of view, it is pertinent to inquire into the prevalance of atypical sexual behavior, on the assumption that it is a measure of sexual maladjustment.

Atypical sexual behavior does not find a congenial setting in Ulithi. Its lack may provide a clue to the extent to which permissiveness, despite controls and frustrations, has brought about what might loosely be called a normal attitude towards sex. "True" homosexuality seems to be unknown. Boys sometimes indulge in mutual masturbation, as do girls, and for this they are scolded and occasionally even beaten by their parents. Women of mature age, usually because of involuntary continence, are said sometimes to resort to mutual masturbation, but only as a substitute for the normal sexual congress being denied them.

Voyeurism and exhibitionism, the latter only among children, are present to a slight degree. Bestiality, necrophilia, sadism, and masochism are completely absent, insofar as can be determined.

Rape, a kind of atypical sexual behavior of a different sort, seems to have been not uncommon in former times but apparently is unknown today. The native definition of rape would have it include the ravishing of both virgins and nonvirgins, the married and the unmarried. The seriousness of the offense varies. In reply to a hypothetical question, it is said that the worst offense would be the ravishment of a married woman. Less serious, in decreasing order, would be the rape of a widow, a virgin, a nonvirginal single woman, and a divorcee. At least these are the responses that informants place on the various possibilities mentioned. Apparently, there is no concept of statutory rape, the rationale being that if consent is given it does not matter what the girl's age may be. In view of the current absence of rape, there is no precise way of measuring social repugnance against it. In the past, it is said, the offender would be greeted with censure and ridicule, but not retaliation. Present-day views can be amusing. One informant, on being asked about the prevalence of forcible coition, simply replied, "But why doesn't the man just ask the girl?" The implication is that he would not be spurned. More telling is a response to a Thematic Apperception Test I administered to 100 persons (one later was deleted for lack of identification of the subject). Of the first 65 persons tested, all interpreted a woodland setting with a man crouched behind a tree and looking at a passing woman carrying plant foods as more or less of a benign scene, usually involving a woman and her husband out gathering food for the family. The artist who drew the picture had tried to suggest in a mild way that this was a situation of potential ravishment. He drew the girl to look attractive, the man evil. Finally, an informant offered the explanation that here was a woman walking through the woods with a bad man hiding behind a tree. The man leaps forward and knocks the woman to the ground—and then steals her food. The answer is not strange, for while we cannot positively document the absence of the idea of rape, we know from the test results that there is far greater concern with food than with sex among the people of the atoll.

8

From Womb to Tomb

Wஹat moulds an individual into a social personality in Ulithi? How does he experience growth, maturity, and final dissolution? The people of the atoll distinguish five epochs in the lifetime of a person: babyhood, childhood, young adulthood, middle age, and old age. Their terminology not only distinguishes all these stages by sex but also gives a label to the status of the individuals in each of these epochs. It should be plain that much thought is given to the phases of the life cycle. And should one look back into the past to consult the brief but perspicacious notations of early commentators, one would be impressed with the constancy in these matters over the years. Storms, epidemics, and conflicts have battered these little islands without effacing a basically enduring pattern of individual development.

Babyhood

Roughly speaking, babyhood encompasses the period of nakedness. A young child dons clothing at the age of five or six, so it is with his life before this event that we are concerned.

A baby is said to belong to both the father and the mother, social recognition of that fact being afforded by an exchange of food between the father's and the mother's families one month after the mother has returned to the menstrual lodge with her baby. The sea is always associated with masculinity, so the man's family presents a gift of fish to the woman's female relatives. After several days or even weeks, these relatives make a return gift of plant foods to the men on the husband's side. No magic and no ritual drama accompany this rite, which, significantly, is not performed for the babies of unmarried mothers. A Ulithian tale, "The Poor Lizard Girl," makes the ritual exchange of food an important part of its plot. It concerns a beautiful girl whose mother was a lizard but whose family was human. The son of a chief falls in love with the girl and succeeds in marrying her, without knowing of her mother's reptilian nature. After a child has been born to the couple, he sends fish to her mother, and in return the lizard solicitously collects plant foods from her own human relatives. She had previously worked just as doggedly to fulfill not only this legitimizing obligation but a similar one required when the couple was married. The story has a happy denouement.

Although during marriage a child belongs to both parents, the father is said to be "more important" to it in many ways. Should there be a divorce, he has custody over the child, regardless of culpability or remarriage. Moreover, the father is more important than the mother in the eventual passing down of usufruct tenure rights to land. But as far as descent is concerned, an opposite situation exists, for a child belongs to the lineage of his mother.

When a child is adopted he belongs in a socio-legal sense to the adoptive parents, but it is very important to know that he continues to be domiciled with his real parents until the age of five to ten, these being the most crucial of the formative years in his life.

The infant is given the breast whenever he cries to be fed or whenever it is considered time to feed him, but sometimes only as a pacifier. He suckles often, especially during the first three to six months of his life, when he may average around eighteen times during the day and night. The great stress placed by Ulithians on food is once more given eloquent expression in nursing practices. Thus, if both the mother and child should happen to be asleep at any time and it seems to someone who is awake that the baby should be fed, both are aroused in order to nurse the baby.

If the mother is alive and well, she ordinarily does all the nursing. However, should her milk be insufficient, a lactating relative on her side of the family is asked to help. A relative on the father's side is usually avoided on the grounds that the baby of that woman, even though he may no longer be feeding at the breast, will be jealous. Such jealousy is not believed to be present on the mother's side. Indeed, on rare occasions, sisters may make an exchange in the nursing of their children.

Because fish and coconuts are thought to be milk producing, a mother eats as much of these as she can. If the first milk is reluctant to issue forth, the flow is stimulated by resorting to medicine or magic. The magic is secretly handed down from mother to daughter, with rare exceptions being made to its secrecy and then only on payment of a substantial gift in exchange for the formula. Jealousy on the part of mothers is assigned as the cause for the reluctance to give such information to persons outside the family. The failure of a mother's milk to flow immediately after childbirth is said to be because the pains and effort of parturition prevent its release, and that the situation will ordinarily be remedied as soon as the mother begins to feel better. No explanation is forthcoming as to why some mothers, even when recovered, are still unable to provide milk for their babies.

Feeding supplementary to nursing begins in a moderate way at the age of two months, at which time the baby may be given coconut cream and a leafless yellow parasitic plant which is first masticated by the mother and then put directly from her mouth into that of the infant. Expanded supplementary feeding begins about the fourth month, although the mother may choose to delay it for several months longer. She usually masticates the foods first and then feeds them to the baby with her fingers.

Weaning begins at varying ages. It is never attempted before the child is a year old, and usually he is much older than that. Some children are suckled until they are five, or even as much as seven or eight. Weaning takes about four days, one technique being to put the juice of hot pepper around the mother's nipples. Physical punishment is never employed, though scolding may be deemed necessary. Ridicule, a common recourse in training Ulithian children, is also resorted to. The child's reaction to being deprived of the breast often manifests itself in temper tantrums. The mother tries to mollify the child, saying that what she is doing is for the best. She may hold the child in a comforting embrace and try to console him by playing with him and offering him such distractions as a tiny coconut or a flower. To increase the little one's interest she may say the object is a tiny baby and that he should take care of it, or she may suggest the object is a canoe. Another way to distract the child is with foods that are especially agreeable to him. The mother tries to heighten the child's desire for the substitute for her breast by verbalizing on the delights of the food. Should these comforting devices fail, the mother may lightly castigate the child, or set him aside to let him cry himself out, although in such an event she remains within sight of the weanling so that he does not feel he has been deserted. As a substitute for the mother's breast, a child is never given anything to suck upon.

The reactions to weaning are not extreme; children weather the crisis well. In fact, a playful element may be observed. A child may quickly push his face into his mother's breast and then run away to play. When the mother's attention is elsewhere, the child may make a sudden impish lunge at the breast and try to suckle from it. After the mother has scolded the weanling, he may coyly take the breast and fondle it, toy with the nipple, and rub the breast over his face. A man told me that when he was being weaned at the age of about seven, he would alternate sleeping with his father and mother, who occupied separate beds. On those occasions when he would sleep with his father, the latter would tell him to say goodnight to his mother. The boy would go over to where she was lying and playfully run his nose over her breasts. She would take this gesture good-naturedly and encourage him by telling him he was virtuous, strong, and like other boys. Then he would go back to his father, satisfied with his own goodness.

The care of the baby is marked by much solicitude on the part of everyone. One of the ways in which this is manifested is through great attention to cleanliness. The infant is bathed three times a day, and after each bath the baby is rubbed all over with coconut oil and powdered with turmeric. Ordinarily, bathing is done by the mother, who, as she holds the child, rocks him from side to side in the water and sings:

> Float on the water,
> In my arms, my arms,
> On the little sea,
> On the big sea,
> The channel sea,
> The rough sea,
> The calm sea,
> On this sea.

Suddenly the mother whisks the baby from the water and makes a quick tossing motion with him, uttering a mock threat,

> Shark! Here is food for you!

The child does not cry at being bathed unless the water is cold, as often it is.

An infant is never left alone. He seems to be constantly in someone's arms, being passed from person to person in order to allow everyone a chance to fondle him. There is not much danger that if neglected for a moment he will harm himself. He cannot fall, for he is already at ground level, where he has been placed to rest. However, safeguards must be maintained against his suffocating, or putting objects in his mouth, or crawling away. He must be protected, too, against inquisitive chickens, dogs, and cats.

A baby should not be taken out of the house at night and carried through the village, for evil spirits will make him ill. If it is imperative that he be taken out after dark, the baby is safeguarded by an amulet over which an incantation has been recited. This kind of magic, already alluded to in Chapter 6, is called "fence" magic because it acts as a barrier in keeping the spirits from seeing the baby or coming into contact with him.

The care of the baby is mostly the concern of the mother. A close female relative is sometimes asked to look after a baby for a while, and, on occasion, the father may mind and feed him, unless the baby is still in the suckling stage. When the child can walk, teen-age children may carry him astride their hips. Mostly they are girls. An infant is usually carried about in a long coconut leaf basket slung from the mother's shoulder.

A sick baby is the cause of great anxiety. Often a practitioner is called in to treat him, but any person may be summoned who has had special experience in dealing with infants' ailments. The most common symptoms of illness are stomach noises and tremors, diarrhea, constipation, vomiting, fever, and rapid pulse. No distinction is made between symptom and disease; that is, the symptom itself is treated, without concern for its ultimate origin. An exception to this attitude occurs in diseases in which spirits have had a hand. For instance, stomach-ache is believed to be due to a spirit. A diviner may be called in to identify the spirit and through his magic he can tell whether it belongs to the category of trees, the sea, or anything else. The diviner then suggests, on the basis of the nature of the spirit implicated, which doctor in the atoll would be most effective in curing the child. Magical therapy may be applied, too, by nonspecialists, such as a mother or relative who knows some magic. In any event, the spell invites the spirit to go away from the baby. One example involves a plea to the demon Hosola, who, it is said, in his great loneliness tries to kill babies so that he may have them for himself.

> May you feel compassion
> O spirit, Hosola,
> Towards this baby.
> Ride, ride away
> On the waves.

But in Ulithi, magic is seldom used without medicine in curing disease, and so we find many concoctions being used, none of which seem to have any real empirical value. It is interesting that the etiology of a disease may often be attributed to the violation by the mother of the taboo against sexual intercourse before the proper lapse of time after parturition.

The great tenderness with which babies are dealt with is again seen when the mother puts her child to sleep. Lullabies are soft and gentle, but most often the songs that are sung are merely dance and love songs with slow rhythms.

The physical development of the child proceeds in a casual way. Folktales, however, often speak of magic applied to heroes to make them grow rapidly—sometimes to manhood in a few days—but the recourse to such means in real life is small. Parents do not like to intervene in a process which they feel will proceed well enough on its own. It is interesting that they do not use "baby talk" when addressing a child, even though they may be amused at the baby's faltering efforts to utter a word and will mimic it with delight.

Toilet training begins late in infancy, not being attempted until the child has some comprehension of what he is being told. The techniques employed consist of punishment, scolding, material rewards, praise, nose rubbing, and conditioning. The person most responsible for toilet training the child is the mother, but his father always stands ready to exert manly pressure when the efforts of the mother go unheeded. Patrilateral relatives are more important than matrilateral ones, allegedly because the baby "belongs" to the father's family. This seems incongruous in a matrilineal society but is insisted upon by the natives.

The feces of an infant are often disposed of by placing them in the hollow of an old tree, the rationale behind this being that otherwise they might be burned by mistake or even maliciously, causing the infant to become ill and perhaps die. When the child has achieved sphincter control he eliminates anywhere near the waterline of the beach, so that when the tide rises it will wash away the excreta. The islets are remarkably free of the odor of urine or fecal matter—eloquent testimony to the inculcation of judicious habits that are carried into adult life. The frequent rains also help. The attitude of the people towards excreta per se is not colored with strong emotions and if there are objections they are based on esthetic rather than moral grounds. Careless or indifferent persons who eliminate near another person's house run the risk of having a concoction placed over their ordure, after which an incantation is recited and the feces burned. The effects: the guilty person's intestines will be permanently forced out of his body. Such magic is only employed when the offender is unknown. When known, the injured party merely forces him to remove the nauseous substance.

The training of the baby, then, is mostly concerned with matters of feeding, speech, locomotion, and elimination; but this is linked with the beginnings of an awareness of sex. It also involves the formation of fundamental patterns in the basic personality of the child, and by the time he is five or six he already has been indelibly oriented into his society. These first years are naturally ones of great concern for the parents and they solicitously do all they can to guide their offspring through to a safer age. Often they are unsuccessful and mortality is high. Should a child die the mortuary rites are the same as for an adult, except that infants are not given formal burial.

Childhood

Childhood is the second stage in the life of the individual, and by native reckoning comes comparatively late. It does not follow immediately upon what we would call infancy, but only after weaning, which we have already noted comes as a long delayed process. The child can now walk, talk, and control elimination. Actually, he has proceeded much beyond all this, for he has now donned clothing and therefore has attained the age of five or six. Boys wear a long grasslike garment made of hibiscus bast that is shredded and made to hang down over the genitals and the buttocks. Girls abandon their nakedness by putting on a bulky "grass" skirt made of shredded coconut leaflets. Children fidget a lot when first they put on clothing and must be trained through scoldings, warnings, and rewards to keep from discarding them.

The education of the child broadens out in earnest during this period. Boys learn how to fish, climb trees for coconuts and palm toddy, make rope, and otherwise assist their elders. Girls learn something about cooking, weeding, gathering wild plants, and how to be of general usefulness to their mothers. However, the learning of economic skills is informal and is gained mostly from observing older people at work. Children are not expected to do a good deal, this being a time when it is thought that their chief concern should be with play.

Sex training is now initiated. The fingering of the genitals is fairly common among both boys and girls and in the course of time usually develops into masturbation, but ceases for the most part with the commencement of coition, usually at the time of puberty. Children are never masturbated by adults. Parents try to keep children from handling their genitals, as well as those of others, but do not always succeed in arousing aversion against it.

The attitude of society is tolerant in matters of sex, and the child soon senses this state of affairs. He comes to realize that the concept of sex is one which should be regarded with modesty rather than guilt. Much latitude is permitted children in hearing about pregnancy and its consequences, and the omnipresent menstrual lodge can scarcely conceal the function which that house serves. Children learn early that premarital coition does not seriously outrage the community, so that when they reach puberty the act is expected. Yet, despite the prevailing tolerance in these matters, avoidances and restraints are exercised. Sexual precocity is regarded with disfavor. A precocious boy is warned that he runs the risk of wasting away his muscles and being unable to resist colds or to grow. The same is said to be true of girls. The objection to sexual precociousness seems due as much as anything else to the disapproval by elders of anything indicative of forwardness. Significantly, the danger of pregnancy does not seem to be raised as a deterrent to the sex act. The one real dread is that a child will violate the strong taboo against incest.

The chief means of actively training the child in matters of sex is through scolding. Should this fail, some kind of punishment is resorted to. Positive sanctions in the form of praise or rewards can scarcely be given, for it is hard to single out an occasion for rewarding a child in such matters. Frequently, adults will make some vague reference to "the spirits" in admonishing a child, without however speaking with much conviction. An ingredient of fear is sometimes injected in different terms, a boy being warned that if he plays with a girl's genital she will bleed, sicken, and die; a girl is warned that if she handles the phallus of a boy he may be injured and perhaps die.

The channelizing of aggression begins in childhood. Aggression often is manifested by a child against his elders through crying and throwing temper tantrums in order to irritate them. For the same reason, he will utter obscene remarks or words, throw stones, or make a commotion. During a tantrum a child may stamp, hit himself on the head with a stone, strike his head against the ground, roll over and over, or merely cry to excess. Often, the real means of expressing aggression is through the mere threat of doing certain things that the child knows the parents object to. He may stand at a distance and taunt them. These threats are made when the child is still so young—five to seven—that the parents will not take excessive umbrage. Although temper tantrums begin back in the period of babyhood, they continue until the child is about eight. The objects of these aggressions are usually the father or mother or, to a lesser extent, an older sibling. The consequences for the child are occasionally advantageous, for he may get his way; but mostly the affair ends in his being punished. A child in a tantrum may simply be ignored by all those about him.

Physical aggression is infrequent among children. Although clashes between them do occur, they strike one another surprisingly little. Fighting takes place mostly at the ages up to eight, and rarely after that. Girls seldom fight with anyone. Boys engaged in a quarrel are quickly separated by other boys or by adults. They are not egged on by other children, who on the contrary may quickly run to tell an adult if a fight has begun.

Aggression manifests itself more commonly in words rather than blows or bites. One child may ridicule a physical defect in another child, or merely hurl obscene words that he has heard others use. Children may even accuse one another of sex play, foul body odors, or dirtiness. Verbal aggression against an adult is not common, and in any event is punished by the adult after a warning, or is reported to the parents if the person offended is not a close relative. The verbal aggressions of children usually cease at about the age of nine; at least, beyond that age they are committed with less frequency and greater caution.

Willful disobedience is infrequent, yet a child may resort to it if he cannot have his way or is forced to do something he does not want to do. He may threaten a parent, saying he will injure, drown, or hang himself, or, perhaps, leave home and become another's child. The results of disobedience are not rewarding, for instead of winning his way the child is almost invariably punished, usually by the mother. Insubordination ends about the age of nine or ten; thereafter, it is virtually absent.

Early in childhood there may be some wanton destruction of property. Small youngsters will scatter things, break baskets and kitchen utensils, and tear apart what they can. Since this sort of display manifests itself when the child is about five and ends when he is about six or seven, it is obviously of short duration. It comes not as the result of brooding or vindictiveness but as a reaction to frustration or scolding.

The person most important in aggression training is the child's mother; next comes the father and the older siblings. When a child is adopted he usually spends his early years with his natural parents, and his adoptive parents consequently do not play a strong role. As a reaction to the control of aggression the child resorts to various outlets, sulking being the most usual, leading occasionally to a general regression. Older children may resort to subterfuge, this being common enough that Ulithians have a name for it. If thumb sucking and nose picking are reactions to training, then they are common in that connection, but there is little fingernail biting and hair twirling. Night terrors are almost unknown, it being said that any crying at night is the result of physical pain of some sort or a desire to eliminate.

Dependency training, already begun of course in infancy, continues throughout the whole period of childhood. The child has previously learned to walk and talk; but children, more as a form of coddling than a means for transporation, are often carried about until they are about six, usually piggyback.

Children play in groups independent of the supervision of adults after they reach the age of five. Their play is spontaneous and carefree, with little competition or aggression. Much time is spent near or in the water, and mothers as well as other adults occasionally cast an anxious eye in their direction and call to them if they venture too far out. Some of the great freedom given to children in their play is because on a small coral islet there are not many hazards, and older children are usually close enough to younger ones so as to be of assistance if necessary. Children play mostly in peer groups, particularly as they grow older, and may even form small cliques. Smaller boys and girls make no special effort to isolate themselves from one another, but older ones do not mingle, except on certain occasions. Children play with adults mostly in connection with certain dances held at night in which everyone participates. They often choose to play in areas where men are lounging about or working in groups, trying sometimes to get recognition from them, but they do not press or sustain their efforts. Indeed, play is so haphazard and relaxed that it quickly melts from one thing to another, and from one place to another, with little inhibition. There is much laughter and chatter, and often some vigorous singing. One gains the impression that relaxation, for which the natives have a word they use almost constantly, is one of the major values of Ulithian culture.

The attitude of society towards unwarranted independence is generally one of disapproval. Normal independence is admired because it leads to later self-reliance in the growing individual, dependence being scorned if it is so strong that it will unfit him for future responsibilities. Ulithians talk a lot about homesickness and do not view this as improper, unless the longing is really for a spouse or a sweetheart, the suspicion here being that it is really sexual outlet that the person wants. Longing of this sort is said to make a person inefficient and perhaps even ill. Homesickness is expected of all children and is not depre- cated. I was greatly touched once when I asked a friend to tell me what a man was muttering about during a visit to my house. He said he felt sad that I was away from my home and friends and wondered how I could endure it. Ulithians do not like people to feel lonely; sociability is a great virtue for them.

The learning of traditional knowledge, beliefs, and values proceeds steadily during childhood. Children spend long sessions with older people and like to listen to them recount stories or just talk about anything. Mention has already been made of the acquiring of technical and economic skills. Elders of course are constantly demanding obedience and respect, and they are quick to deprecate shouting and foul language. Older people will not tolerate running through the village paths or trespassing in tabooed areas. They scorn crying and forbid quarreling in their presence. Begging is intolerable. Honesty is insisted upon with almost a passion. All in all the standards of behavior are simple and always moderate. Fortunately, the training of the child is in such harmony with these ideals that there is a minimum of discrepancy between expected and actual behavior.

Adulthood

The mild concerns of ordinary life begin to catch up with the individual in the early years of adulthood and he can never again revert to the joyful indif- ference of his childhood.

Attaining adulthood is marked by a ritual for boys and another for girls, neither of which is featured by genital operations. The same term, *kufar,* is used for each of the initiations.

The boy's *kufar* is much the less elaborate and important. It comes about when he begins to show secondary sex characteristics and is marked by three ele- ments: a change to adult clothing, the performance of magic, and the giving of a feast. All this occurs on the same day. The boy changes from the long grass- like hibiscus "skirt" to the banana fiber breechclout of men. This is followed by a rite performed by one of the parents, or any relative or friend knowing the formula, in which an incantation is recited over the youth, while at the same time two young coconut leaflets, tied at their ends, are snapped together before his face. The chant is designed to bring good luck to the adolescent in his choice of a mate and in his marriage. Upon completion of the incantation, the leaves, which are categorized as a talisman by the natives, are placed around the boy's neck for him to wear a day or more before hanging it in his house for an indefinite period of time. The feast follows the magic and is merely a small domestic affair, joined in by all the members of the immediate family except the youth's sisters, who are forbidden not only to share in the food but even to witness the rite. The boy undergoes no hazing or tests of manliness.

The outstanding consequence of the boy's ritual is that he must now sleep in the men's house and scrupulously avoid his postpubertal sisters. Not only may he not sleep in the same house with them, but he and they may not walk together, share the same food, touch one another's personal baskets, wear one another's leis or other ornaments, make or listen to ribald jokes in one another's presence, watch one another when doing a solo dance, or listen to one another sing a love song. The youth is expected to prevent anyone in a mixed group from using obscene words in a sister's presence. If a man and his sister have even to approach one another, the woman must give warning that she is coming close by, and when she passes her brother she must do this in the crouched position of respect used towards superior and elders. There is no further seclusion from women than this.

The *kufar* for girls is much more prolonged and important than that for boys, having two aspects, one of which signifies the physiological coming of age and the other the sociological attainment of adulthood. The onset of the menarche has unusual importance because of the great preoccupation manifested by Ulithians towards the catemenial discharge. A woman spends about a fourth or more of her procreative life in isolation from her husband and the community. Conversely, the effects of the catemenial cycle are inevitably felt by the men, who must make compensatory adjustments in their own behavior. Extraordinary precautions are especially taken to see that a menstruating woman does not ritually contaminate magico-religious specialists. Indeed, she must avoid all men, and to insure this she is confined to a menstrual house until three days have elapsed after the completion of her period. Men are strictly forbidden to trespass on the grounds surrounding the house, except in the event of grave emergency.

As soon as the girl notices the first flow of blood she knows she must immediately repair to the women's house. The current inmates have usually had some warning of the event, and as she approaches they all chant slowly but loudly enough for the village to hear: "The menstruating one, ho-o-o! The menstruating one, ho-o-o!" Other women, hearing the commotion, may come from all directions to join the chanting. Certainly, no attempt is made to conceal the event; indeed, someone may race through the village announcing it to everyone within hearing. It is interesting that the chanting of the women is said to keep the spirits from sending rain, since menstruation is somehow related to sea spirits and the weather.

The first act of the girl after entering the lodge is to take a bath, still clothed in her grass skirt, in the lagoon near the house. She then changes this skirt for a dry one. At the same time she places a wrap-around skirt on top of her head, for should she fail to do this it is said that the sun would become so hot that everything would be scorched. For four days she goes about with the skirt folded on her head, after which she transfers it to her shoulders for another four days, and then sets it aside. There then follows the same kind of magic used to initiate boys into adulthood. Her mother or, if she does not know the words, a close female relative will recite a spell designed to bring good luck in finding a mate and enjoying a happy married life. As the words are intoned, young coconut leaves, *ubwoth,* are snapped before the girl's eyes. The leaves are a talisman and are worn for a day or more, and then hung up near her sleeping quarters. It is in connection with this phase of the long rite that the change to adult clothing occurs.

On the first day of the girl's confinement the special dance called the *hamath,* already alluded to in connection with institutionalized ridicule, is performed by men dancing in the village and women on the grounds of the lodge. The girl does not participate. The dances are begun during the day and resumed at night, the alleged purpose being to prevent the coming of a typhoon. Ordinarily, this dance may not be witnessed by persons of the opposite sex, the only other exceptions being in connection with criticism and with catching turtles.

The newly initiated girl must observe many taboos that not only restrict her movements but forbid her to cook her own meals, eat with other people, or touch their food. These *etap* keep her from coming in contact with men and at the same time separate her to a great extent from other women confined to the house. To assist in keeping the taboos, a prepubertal girl becomes her constant companion and assistant for a long period of time, doing her cooking and other chores. She alone is exempt from the prohibition of eating with the initiated girl.

After the initiate has been in the menstrual lodge for eight days, some *etap* are lifted by a rite of the same kind generally used to lift other taboos in Ulithi. It is performed either by a diviner or a typhoon magician. The magician does not perform his rite in the presence of the girl, for she is strongly taboo to him. He does it in the safety of his house, using two kinds of leaves tied into two bundles. After reciting the incantation over them, in which he beseeches the spirits to relieve the girl of the taboos, he sends the bundles to the menstrual house, where a woman, any at all, takes them and waves them in a circle around the head of the seated or standing girl. Henceforth, she may have more freedom of movement in the grounds about the house, and she may do her own cooking. All the other taboos imposed on the first day remain in force as long as the girl stays at the house. To celebrate the lifting of the taboos, raw food contributed by her relatives is distributed in her honor, but none of the primary magico-religious specialists may partake of it—so potentially dangerous to them is any association with catemenial impurity.

The girl ends her confinement when six days have elapsed since the taboo-lifting rite—fourteen days after she first entered. She lives in a private hut of her own, built for her near her parents' house, her young companion staying there with her. Most taboos still remain in force and cause her to avoid not only men but often women as well. The hut is not a substitute for the menstrual house, to which she must repair whenever her discharge begins. While in the women's house she has greater restrictions than older women who are not newly initiated, being given more freedom only after she has completed ten confinements. After a total of twelve confinements, she has the same status as other women at the house, but not when she leaves it to return to the village. During a period of three years after her first menstrual discharge she may not go near any of the primary magicians, and must wait ten years in all before she may even touch one of them, unless she is married to him. This is usually unlikely because of the relatively greater age at which men of this sort are admitted to their profession.

Adolescence and adulthood come rushing together at young Ulithians, and the attitude of the community towards them undergoes a rapid change. The boy and the girl are admitted to a higher status, to be sure, and they are given certain rights and listened to with more respect when they speak. But a good deal is expected of them in return. Young men bear the brunt of the heaviest tasks assigned by the men's council. For their own parents they must help build and repair houses, carry burdens, climb trees for coconuts, fish, make rope, and perform all the other tasks commonly expected of an able-bodied man. Young women are similarly called upon to do much of the harder work of the village and the household. Older people tend to treat these very young adults with a sudden sternness and formality lacking when they were in their childhood. The missteps of young people are carefully watched and readily criticized, so that new adults are constantly aware of the critical gaze of their elders. They may not voice strong objections or opinions, and have no political rights whatsoever, accepting the decisions of the men's and women's councils without murmur. Altogether, they are suddenly cut off from children and must undergo a severe transition in their comportment towards others about them. Only in the amatory sphere can they find release from the petty tyranny of their elders.

Marriage is permitted upon reaching adolescence but is usually deferred for a few years, during which the young man or woman is free to carry on premarital sex relations. Marriage is considered to be the natural condition for every adult, there seldom being any individuals who never marry at all. If a man were to avoid marriage, it would be said that he is both selfish and lazy.

A romantic kind of love often enters into the selection of a mate, especially the first. Good appearance is one of the foremost ideals, but the possibility of finding a handsome mate is often limited by reason of the small population and the rules of incest. Industry, kindness, and compatibility are esteemed virtues. Wealth is a secondary consideration; indeed, it is hardly a consideration at all, since there is little inequality in this respect. Marriage to the son or daughter of a chief is not especially sought after as it confers no extra rights or rank in a matrilineal society. Aside from the limitations imposed by the hard rules of incest, there are few restrictions on marriage. Insanity is the chief obstacle, followed by some great physical handicap. Ulithians marry freely within or without their villages. They often find spouses outside the atoll, except for Yap, where it is not permitted to marry into these higher "caste" classes.

It is after the several liaisons that come before marriage that a boy and girl discover that they have a deeper interest in one another than one based on sexual relations alone. They may express their interest through a series of small gifts exchanged informally. The decision to marry is not forced by pregnancy; indeed, the boy has no obligations if his sweetheart becomes gravid. No serious stigma attaches to the illegitimate child or its mother, and there are always those eager to care for both. The child is adopted before it is born, and the mother has no difficulty in finding a husband.

The initiation of marriage negotiations, then, arises out of the probings so freely permitted young people. The initiative rests with the boy, although exceptions occur when the girl is particularly ardent. Only seldom do parents arrange marriages; they ordinarily give consent to what is practically an accomplished fact. On rare occasions a couple may find it necessary to elope.

There is no wedding ceremony. As soon as the young couple have decided to marry, they arrange to sleep together, and the public demonstration of their intent is made known to everyone by simple cohabitation. Postnuptial events are few. A few days or even a month after the marriage, the groom's family puts turmeric on the body of the girl and dresses her in a new skirt. Several weeks later, his family goes fishing and donates the catch to the girl's family, and the latter divides the fish among lineage mates on both sides. The gesture is not one-sided, for the girl's family makes a return gift of plant foods at the same time it receives the fish.

There is no bar to polygyny and occasionally there are marriages of this sort, but for the most part such marriages are considered so impractical economically that it does not enter into a man's mind to take on another spouse. There are no moral considerations involved. Aside from the need for a man to be possessed of enough "muscle," as one native put it, to supply two wives and their children with food, he would also have to be endowed with enough "smartness" to keep harmony within the family. The customs of the levirate and sororate are occasionally carried out, however, without being enjoined.

A marriage is crowned with success if a wife becomes pregnant and bears a child. The desire for children is strong. One might take the skeptical view that the desire for children is motivated by economic considerations, but this would ignore the obvious delight that a man and a woman take in having young ones about them. No preference exists for a baby of a particular sex, except in individual instances; people think in terms of wanting babies rather than wanting a boy or a girl. Sometimes women resort to magic or take a medicine to induce pregnancy, but the belief in their efficacy is not sustained by the results. No effort to prevent conception is made, and the people say it would be ludicrous to control birth, for it would deprive parents of the great comfort a child can bring to them. Consistent with this attitude is the acceptance of twin births as a fortunate turn of affairs rather than a matter of regret, for here the mother has a double share of happiness.

The pregnant woman is treated with solicitude. In a world in which food taboos seem to be ubiquitous, it comes as a surprise to find that not only is she not placed under any restrictions but is on the contrary allowed anything she desires. There is a cultural pattern whereby she is asked to express some special preference, and she may say she wants a pig, chicken, certain fish, or anything else not ordinarily a part of her diet. In actual practice the food she gets is distributed as a gift among her relatives. For this reason, the granting of this pregnancy wish is really not the gratification of a real food craving as much as it is another one of those countless occasions that serve as a distributive mechanism for food. If the woman has a real craving, it is catered to in routine fashion.

The lack of taboos surrounding the gravid woman's food extends to all other areas of life, with two exceptions. She may not enter the sacred swamp garden or have coitus once past the first three or four months of pregnancy. Yet, as if to emphasize the concern of her relatives, they are not allowed to carry on activities connected with canoe or house building, and may not eat any of the food supplied while the canoe or house is being built or when a feast is given at their completion. Her husband's relatives have lesser taboos in the same context. This is not to imply that not enough is being done to see the woman to a successful termination of her condition. In view of the perilous character of parturition, she is given medicines to help her in a general way and other medicines to make delivery easy. Miscarriages are believed to result either from natural causes—overstraining, fright, corporal injury—as well as supernatural ones—violation of any of the taboos associated with pregnancy. A woman who has had a miscarriage must retire to the menstrual house and remain three full moons, just as if the baby had been born and lived. The dead foetus is buried in simple fashion in a hole on the menstrual house grounds.

Abortion, like the prevention of conception, is not practiced. This can be explained in part by the tolerant attitude toward illegitimate births, and in part by the great desire for children. Moreover, there is no feeling that babies will tie down a woman, obstruct her extramarital amours, or reduce her desirability as a sexual partner. As for infanticide, there is not any evidence whatsoever that it has ever existed in Ulithi.

Unless unusual circumstances interfere, parturition always takes place in the menstrual house. Should labor begin unexpectedly and the woman delivers her child away from the house, this not only is not considered an ill omen but instead a fortunate circumstance that shortens the period of waiting. The ancestral ghosts are said to have intervened in favor of the woman.

At the menstrual house, the expectant mother is assisted by everyone present. She now observes a food taboo for the first time; it forbids her to eat food grown in the swamp garden. When delivery approaches, all children are cleared out of the area. Women experienced in these matters, but not "professionally" trained, help in the delivery; most commonly it is the girl's mother who plays the chief role. Labor is facilitated by massage and the use of native medicines. Respiration in the newborn babe is induced by massaging the arms and legs in a direction always towards the trunk. The head, too, is massaged, and should all this fail, an attendant will put water in her mouth and spray it on the head of the infant. The umbilical cord and afterbirth are buried in the grounds of the house near the beach. Should a woman die in labor, the child is given to a lactating relative to nourish. Maternal mortality is high.

Unusual births are not common, nor is there much speculation regarding them. A caul birth is said to be due to the disregard of the mother for the avoidance of fishnets. It has no other significance, good or bad. Triple and other multiple births beyond twins are claimed never to have occurred within the memory of any living inhabitants. Twins of course are welcomed.

The new mother must spend three full moons at the menstrual house, and during this time the father may not see his offspring. The woman is under no taboos, although other women are forbidden to trespass upon her sleeping quarters. She is expected to devote all her energies towards the care of her baby. During her confinement, she never drinks ordinary water—only water from the coconut. Other women try to be of service at every turn.

After three full moons have elapsed, the mother goes home with her child. She is expected to avoid strenuous exertion, for otherwise this will make her infant sick and "the spirits" will be angered. At this time a severe taboo is placed on her having any sexual relations with her husband, so she does not even sleep with him. It is not until the child is able to walk unassisted to the beach and duck his head in the water that marital relations may be resumed. It takes as long as four years for this to happen, so that any intercourse before then must be avoided to keep the child from becoming sick and dying. However, the father may have relations with other women without harm to the baby if the child sleeps apart from both the parents. An examination of census records shows that the spacing of a woman's children does not conform to the taboo, and for this there are several possible reasons. Discounting the fact that the taboo has lately been less operative than it used to be, it is likely that the woman either has broken the rule against relations with her husband or has engaged in adulterous affairs. As far as I could ascertain, there is no societal rule against her having sexual relations with someone other than her husband—at least, no more than would be the case if her child were beyond the early developmental stage.

Sterility or barrenness never constitute grounds for divorce, but adultery, frigidity, sexual incompatibility, desire to marry another person, desertion, laziness, failure to fulfill economic obligations, thievery, and insanity are sufficient for either spouse. A man may divorce a wife who attempts to conceal her menses in order to avoid going to the menstrual house. Conjugal infidelity is not as overpowering a reason for divorce as in many societies. While the dissolution of marriages is easy and common, and without formal procedure, it tends to occur early in the first marriage before any children are born. Most Ulithians get married about three times.

A divorced couple has to make certain adjustments. The spouse on whose lineage land the house in which they have been living has been built retains residence there, and the other spouse, most often the wife, leaves to live with his or her family. In practice, the unmarried man must actually sleep in his home. He must take up sleeping quarters in the *metalefal,* where all other unmarried men are required to stay. There is no penalty against a guilty party in a divorce. However, the first of the spouses to remarry must pay a gift to the ex-spouse. Should that party and his or her relatives not make the payment, the relatives of the aggrieved party are entitled to arrive en masse at the home of the delinquent and confiscate anything in sight. No protest is made and no resistance is offered because public opinion is outraged by failure to make the gift payment. It is interesting that when the second spouse remarries, no gift indemnity is made. The need to pay compensation is apparently not designed to prevent a hasty divorce, and in any event does not accomplish such a result even if so intended.

The children of a divorced couple do not suffer harshly. Although the father has technical custody, in practice they live with the mother, with occasional residence with the father. A woman who is divorced while pregnant has full claim on the child born to her. It is unusual, however, for a man to terminate a marriage under such circumstances since for selfish reasons he may want to claim the child as his, which he cannot do if he is divorced before the child is born. The maintenance of a child whose parents have terminated their marriage is up to the persons with whom the offspring is living.

Avoidance between divorced couples is mostly a personal decision, and the two parties may even be friendly enough to have sexual connections. They must, however, in any event avoid one another's families. Eventually, the ill feeling engendered by a divorce may be eroded and friendly relations on the part of all concerned may be renewed. In view of the smallness of the community and the frequency of divorce, it would be impractical for divorced couples and their respective families to maintain a permanent grudge.

The ever-running years advance these young people through later adulthood into middle age, the fourth period in the Ulithian division of life.

There are no criteria of middle age beyond the silent touches of time, when the physiological transformations that come at the end of the fourth decade can be noted. For a woman, this fourth stage is not necessarily connected with the ushering in of the menopause, which in any event is not marked by either a rite or other symbol. As with a man, the signs are the beginning of loss of muscle tonus, the appearance of graying, and all the little indicators that a people must employ when they do not count the years. Almost every man and woman has been married by this time. Bachelorhood and spinsterhood are deviant statuses, forced on individuals only by mental or physical disability. A widow or widower, or even a person divorced, is under pressure to remarry as soon as possible, if only for predominantly economic reasons.

The middle-aged person commands the respect of all those younger than himself and wields authority over them. This is especially true when he or she has become a member of the men's or women's council, a status not inevitably attained, however, by everyone. The elders keep younger people in check mostly through criticism and ridicule, as well as occasional threats. Young adults must show their deference by bending down as they pass in front of them, uttering the formulistic words, *"Soro! Soro!"*

In their evaluation of the personality of the middle-aged individual, Ulithians are guided by certain standards. The ideal man is, first of all, industrious and capable in the arts of men. He is intelligent, handsome, muscular, and healthy, as well as faithful, honest, cooperative, kind, jovial, and impartial. Such a man loves his family and has fathered many children. Neither wealth, lineage, nor political position are important or necessary in the Ulithian concept of what a man should be like.

The ideal woman, more than anything else, is industrious. She is intelligent, too. She obeys her husband, caters to his wishes, and remains ever faithful to him. She is pleasant and sociable, and neither gossips nor creates friction. She is attractive and healthy, but not too robust, for this would detract from her charms as a woman. She is fond of children and has raised a large family. It is not necessary that she belong to a particular lineage, or possess many rights to land. The status of an adult woman is lower than that of a man, but in practice she may take the initiative from her husband in many subtle ways. By force of personality, a woman may make her wishes felt in the men's council by influencing her husband, who then follows her suggestions at meetings. However, he would never admit to himself or anyone else that she had swayed him.

Middle-aged people may lean heavily on the younger in economic and technological activities but they still have much to occupy them. Aside from attending council meetings, a man is expected to aid in gardening and other small chores. Although he makes no effort to keep up with the young men, he still goes out fishing or climbs coconut trees. He spends more time than before in lounging at the men's house or a canoe shed, but while there and conversing with his friends he justifies himself by working leisurely at making rope, parts of a loom, fishhooks, and the like. Nothing strenuous, but enough to avoid criticism. A middle-aged woman spends her time in the area of her hut, engaged either in some domestic chore or tending small children while their mothers are away. She also is expected to continue with light gardening. Women do not seem to have the leisure of men, but when they are engaged in work their efforts are by comparison more desultory and slower-paced. They sit on the ground a good deal, legs extended before them, and I have more than once remarked that when a Ulithian woman reaches middle age she seems rooted to the ground, never again to regain her feet unless absolutely necessary. It is mostly in the realm of the supernatural that a woman has highest standing, and then only in a limited sense. A woman is excluded from practicing the magic of the more prestigeful arts, but she is allowed to learn many of their techniques in order to pass them on to her sons. She is, however, allowed to practice the healing art, with all that this implies for the manipulation of supernatural forces. She can work sorcery and countermagic, and make amulets and good luck pieces. Much of the minor magic of everyday life, including that associated with the puberty rites of boys and girls, may be exercised by her. A middle-aged woman may even be a medium, but always for a female ghost—never a male.

Middle age ends approximately at the termination of the sixth decade of life. Because men suffer from a greater rate of mortality, they are clearly outnumbered by women of this age period.

The years, as a writer once said, may steal fire from the mind and vigor from the limb, but Ulithians consider that on the whole middle age is the best time of life. It is then that a person enjoys the most stability and the greatest prestige in the community, as well as the strongest authority. Mental and physical faculties have not yet declined to the low ebb of old age.

Senescence and Death

Old age is dreaded not so much because people do not want to die but because they do not want to live to be senile dependents. Sickness is feared when it means the termination of life for a man who is still in control of his senses, with perhaps many years of vigorous participation ahead; but sickness is not dreaded so much in old age, for it can always be cured by death. When death comes, people meet it with all the palliatives at their command. They are not introspective about it; they do not brood.

This last stage of life is not, by native standards, a good period, for it is then that people are ugly, mentally clouded, inactive and dependent. So distasteful is the contemplation of senility that people would rather die in their late sixties or early seventies than continue on in a helpless and childlike condition. As people grow old, they long for some way of rejuvenating themselves, but they have no theories or procedures for bringing about such an effect. Even the traditional narrative has no stories regarding the renewal of youth.

The aged earnestly desire to be of service, and consequently many of them carry on activities with the vigor of the middle-aged. Chieftains may perform their administrative duties in addition to gardening, weeding, carpentry, and fishing. I knew of a high chief who was regarded as indolent, but I discovered he was about eighty-four years of age. It was pointed out in rebuttal that an old man on Falalop continued to make himself useful, even though he was about ninety-two. Aged women may similarly continue to perform domestic duties and attend to babies.

Within the household, the authority of the aged is not challenged by the younger men and women. They may continue to give orders concerning the running of the household. In the men's council, old men may exercise even greater power and authority than when they were only middle-aged. The opinions of old men and women must always be listened to and not deprecated as the babblings of people who have outlived their usefulness. However, in matters of training and disciplining the young, they yield to others, except for an occasional expression of advice or criticism. They are very indulgent toward children, but less indulgent towards persons past puberty.

The ones chiefly responsible for the care and support of the aged are their children, who make every sacrifice to ease their condition. Aged couples do not always live under the same roof with their children, preferring to have their own houses, to which sons and daughters come and spend considerable time with them, moving in if necessary. At any rate, parents do not forsake their own houses in order to move in with their children. Should they have no children, a relative would fill the role of caretaker and provider. In Ulithi, this is not a problem, as a person always seems to have at least a few relatives. I once inquired into this matter and was told that only in one instance could it be recalled where an aged person had had no kinsmen. This concerned an old woman who had outlived all her relatives, including everyone in her lineage, but others stepped in to look after her.

When one is so stricken with age that death hovers about, he is granted any favors he may wish. Any pronouncements he may make regarding the disposal of his body and property are respectfully listened to, and there is no air of incredulity or indifference. A dying man or woman is surrounded by all the relatives who can betake themselves to his house, even if they have to travel long distances from other islands beyond the atoll. I have observed relatives, especially older ones, remaining for weeks and even months at the side of a person believed to be near death.

Ulithians feel that ordinarily death comes to the aged as the result of natural causes and not, as with younger people, because of sorcery, taboo violation, or the hostility of spirits of ghosts. The cessation of life is detected by touching the abdomen just below the ensiform process, and if there is no movement this is a sign the soul has left. There is a relationship between the soul and breath. With the last breath the soul leaves the body, usually through the top of the head, but through the legs if the last breath is exhaled rather than inhaled. In either event, it goes from the body and hovers about on earth for a brief time.

After four days the corpse is interred and the soul flies away to the island of Angaur in the Palaus, where it takes a bath. Notions regarding the particulars vary, but in general Angaur is not a place of tribulation. Rather it is a mere stopping point along the journey to Lang, the Sky World. Though Lang is in the heavens it is not a pleasant place for all. A decision is made regarding the ultimate fate of the soul, this being left up to the great god, Ialulep. Those who have led unsatisfactory lives are consigned to a place known alternatively as Gum Well or Garbage Well, infested by such obnoxious animals as eels and snakes. Here the ghost must remain forever, being unable to escape because of the stickiness of the gum in which it wallows.

Ialulep rewards the worthy by sending them to either of two paradises, one of which is in the northern half of the afterworld, the other in the southern. It is not known by informants why the god decides in favor of one against the other, since both are equally delightful. There are no troubles; people are continuously happy, spending all their time dancing and playing. Marriage is permitted and babies are conceived and born, as in earthly life. It seems incongruous for a people whose lives are so focussed on eating that ghosts feed only on the leaves and flowers of plants, as well as the fragrance that they emit. New arrivals are feted by old residents so as to relieve them of homesickness and any desire to return to earth to see their relatives.

But ghosts may, and do, return to earth for visits. People cannot see them, detecting their presence only when they possess a person and cause him to transmit their words. The experience of possession is the only direct contact which mortals have with ghosts. For this reason relatives watch out for visits from the departed. Before a person is actually possessed he receives a warning in which the ancestor enters him momentarily and instructs him to prepare certain gifts, such as loincloths, turmeric, and wreaths. The ghost then returns to Lang, where it remains for four days. In the meantime, the family of the individual who has received this warning eagerly prepares the gifts and deposits them in a special spot in the house reserved for this purpose. On the first day the gifts are deposited; on the second, third, and fourth, wreaths are left in the morning and in the evening. All during this four-day period of preparation and expectation, the relative who has been selected as his medium feels ill, and his family makes wreathes for him and sings a song for him. This is done in order to gain the favor of the ghostly ancestor so that when it speaks it will reveal valuable information. When possession finally occurs, the medium may be caught unawares. He may be sleeping, eating, or walking. To be sure, he has usually ingested a concoction to induce possession, but he never can be sure of the time when the ghost will actually visit him. During a seance he loses consciousness of all about him and trembles throughout his whole body. This continues for an hour or two, during which time the ancestor, who may be only a child, reveals what he has to say.

Our digression into the career of the dead ancestor's soul has led us away from the living who have been attending the dying person before final dissolution. They have gathered about. They have summoned doctors and magicians, and appealed in final desperation to Marespa or ancestral ghosts of their own lineage to postpone death. They have listened to the admonishments of the sinking individual to younger people: be honest with one another, come to one another's aid when in need, and live in harmony. During his last moments, if the dying person has taught any of the sacred professions or arts to others, he will be visited by his living pupils, who come into his room and recite formal requests for the ghost of the dying person to help them afterwards in the exercise of their work.

When death finally comes, relatives and friends set up a formalized wail. The songs of lamentation are not created for the specific occasion but are traditional songs handed down from some incident in the more remote past. The dirges are deeply moving laments, and even though they are ritualistically determined they are sincere and motivated by a real sense of loss. I have had women sing songs of lamentation for me in order to record them, and the memories aroused have been so keen that the women have shed copious tears.

The corpse is washed, covered with turmeric, and decorated with flower garlands about the neck and head. Sometimes a portion of the deceased's head hair is cut off as a souvenir by a close relative and is stored in a wooden box. Ulithians are great sentimentalists. The corpse is always disposed of by interment, and must be wrapped in a special mat kept handy by a family for any such eventuality.

The preparation of the grave is attended with many taboos and much magic, some of which has already been described briefly. The funeral procession and the actual burial follow a good deal of ritual procedure and symbolism. The head of the corpse is always placed at the lagoon side of the island, with legs extended. In the right arm of the deceased are placed a loincloth and turmeric, so he can present them as gifts to the custodian at the entrance of the other world as soon as he reaches there. Grave goods are placed with the dead person; these consist of some of his or her personal belongings, such as knives, coconut graters, cups, bowls, sleeping mats, loincloths, combs, necklaces, and the like. Gifts brought by relatives and friends, as well as persons using the deceased's land on loan, are also buried with the dead.

For three days lamentations continue at the grave, and on the fourth a permanent stone slab memorial in the shape of a four-sided tomb is erected over the grave. The slabs are bulky and heavy, and are cut with great difficulty from the coral bed of the reef. The next day the soul leaves the earth and begins its journey to Lang, this being on the fifth day (but only after the lapse of four full days).

Cemeteries are numerous and are located along the lagoon. At one time burials were alongside the houses, allegedly to alleviate the grief of the survivors, for then the deceased would somehow be close by. Burial places are not weeded or otherwise tended to because of a taboo against trespass, except on the occasion of a new burial. They are also avoided because of the fear of certain demons who appear at night in various forms, such as balls of fire, and can be heard moaning. They are not the ghosts of the dead but malevolent spirits living in the graveyards.

The period of mourning varies according to circumstances. In any event, the whole village observes a ten-day period of respect, when everyone must comport himself with appropriate decorum. No one may laugh, shout, dance, wash too freely, or put on adornments. Mourning is more stringent for close relatives, however, and they observe certain practices for five full lunar months: no sexual relations, no entering the sacred garden or eating of food grown in it, no entering the men's house, and so on. Men and women must cut off all their hair.

Those who have washed the corpse and dug the grave are under even greater restrictions and for a longer period of time. They must sleep in special quarters away from all others for a period of ten days and otherwise keep segregated from the rest of the village, especially men belonging to the more important categories of supernatural practice. The taboos they observe are designed to keep from contaminating others with the effects of contact with the corpse.

Finally, when close relatives have ended their five-month period of mourning, a rite called "pay stone" is held to reward those who rendered services in connection with the funeral. In practice, all the village is invited to participate in the distribution of food prepared by the close relatives of the deceased. The food, both cooked and raw, is not eaten on the spot but taken home for consumption. A variant of the "pay stone," known as the "think chief," is held when mourning is ended for a chief.

Death is not complete dissolution for the Ulithian. While the name of the dead person may not be mentioned by relatives and friends, his or her memory is not effaced. For a while it is preserved through sentiment, taboo, and ritual; more lastingly, it endures through the system of ancestor worship. Ghosts come back to visit their loved ones and even guide their lives. Although death often strikes harshly at children, women in labor, or men at sea, and disease always lurks at every door, the people are not morbid or defeated by death. Their rituals afford them some victories and their mythology the hope for a happy life in another realm. Though their gods are somewhat distant they assure that the world has an enduring structure, and their ancestral ghosts stand by to give more immediate aid when it is merited. So, after their bereavements, they spring back resiliently into their lives of work and exuberant enjoyment of life. They do not retreat.

Glossary

AFFINAL: Related by marriage.

AMULET: An object that gives supernatural protection for the possessor.

CASTE: A division of society into which nonmembers may not marry.

CLAN: An allegedly consanguineal, unilinear group whose members trace descent through an imaginary ancestor (usually a totem).

COGNATIC: The relationship between people who share ancestry traced through both males and females.

COMMENSAL UNIT: A group that customarily eats together.

CONSANGUINEAL: Related by "blood" or common ancestry.

CORPORATE: Referring to a body of individuals having an identity over and above its individual members and capable of succession.

CROSS-COUSINS: The children of one's father's sister or one's mother's brother.

DISTRAINT: An act, usually involving the seizure of property, designed to insure that an offender will compensate for a wrong.

EGO: The designator in the naming of relatives by their kin terms, or the reference point in discussing them.

EXOGAMY: A rule or practice whereby marriage takes place outside a given group.

KINDRED: A kin group composed of the consanguineal relatives on both the father's and mother's side.

LINEAGE: A unilinear consanguineal kin group which traces descent through known genealogical ties.

MAGIC: A complex of beliefs and techniques for manipulating supernatural power.

MATRILINEAL: The mother-daughter line of descent determining the inheritance of kin membership, property, and authority.

PATRILINEAL: The father-son line of descent determining the inheritance of kin membership, property, and authority.

PATRILOCAL: Involving residence in or near the dwelling of a groom's parents.

POLYGYNY: The marriage of one man to more than one woman.

RITUAL: Those forms of prescribed formal behavior which have no direct technological consequence and are symbolic.

SIBLING: A brother or sister, irrespective of sex. Ulithians designate siblings according to whether they are of the same sex as Ego or of opposite sex.

Taboo: A sacred prohibition whose violation entails usually vague supernatural sanctions.

Talisman: An object that produces supernatural effects of advantageous character for the possessor.

Unilinear: Traced through either a male or a female line of descent.

Recommended Reading

DAMM, HANS, et al., Zentralkarolinen, Part 2 (Ifaluk, Aurepik, Sorol, Mogemog). *Ergebnisse der Südsee-Expedition, 1908–1910.* Hamburg Wissenschaftliche Stiftung und Deutsche Forschungsgemeinschaft. Hamburg: Friederichsen, De Gruyter and Co., 1938.

The section on Mogmog covers the work of Paul Hambruch on Ulithi for a two-week period in 1909. Although the emphasis is topical, there are invaluable records and texts, as well as fine drawings and photographs.

LESSA, WILLIAM A., "Ulithi and the Outer Native World," *American Anthropologist,* 52:27–52, 1950.

A detailed analysis of the place of Ulithi in the Yap empire.

———, "Depopulation on Ulithi," *Human Biology,* 27:161–183, 1955.

A census of Ulithi as of 1949, with implications for depopulation.

———, "Myth and Blackmail in the Western Carolines," *Journal of the Polynesian Society,* 65:66–74, 1956.

An effort to correct the suggestion that Yap's hold on her satellites arises from fears inspired by myth.

———, "Divining from Knots in the Carolines," *Journal of the Polynesian Society,* 68:188–204, 1959.

The great role of knot divination is described for the Carolines.

———, "Tales from Ulithi Atoll: A Comparative Study of Oceanic Folklore." Berkeley and Los Angeles: *University of California Publications: Folklore Studies,* 13, 1961.

A vast analysis of certain Ulithian tales and motifs, and their cognates throughout all of Oceania, with attention to cultural influences.

———, "The Decreasing Power of Myth on Ulithi," *Journal of American Folklore,* 75:153–159, 1962.

Acculturation is seen as causing myth to lose political authority.

———, "An Evaluation of Early Descriptions of Carolinian Culture," *Ethnohistory,* 9:313–403, 1962.

The anthropological value of virtually everything written on the Carolines before 1850 is examined.

———, "The Social Effects of Typhoon Ophelia (1960) on Ulithi," *Micronesica,* 1:1–47, 1964.

How a devastating typhoon hastened incipient social change in Ulithi.

———, and TRACY LAY, "The Somatology of Ulithi Atoll,"

American Journal of Physical Anthropology, 11:405–412, 1953.

Measurements and observations on 59 male Ulithians are reported.

————, and GEORGE C. MYERS, "Population Dynamics of an Atoll Community," *Population Studies,* 15:244–257, 1962.

The significance of a 1960 census of Ulithi for population increase.

————, and MARVIN SPIEGELMAN, "Ulithian Personality as Seen through Ethnological Materials and Thematic Test Analysis." Berkeley and Los Angeles: *University of California Publications in Culture and Society,* 2 (5), 1954.

A description of Ulithian personality traits as seen from an analysis of 99 TAT protocols and from field observation.